OVERSIGHT

OVERSIGHT

REPRESENTING THE INTERESTS OF BLACKS AND LATINOS IN CONGRESS

Michael D. Minta

PRINCETON UNIVERSITY PRESS   PRINCETON AND OXFORD

Copyright © 2011 by Princeton University Press

Published by Princeton University Press, 41 William Street, Princeton, New Jersey 08540
In the United Kingdom: Princeton University Press, 6 Oxford Street, Woodstock,
Oxfordshire OX20 1TW
press.princeton.edu

Library of Congress Cataloging-in-Publication Data

Minta, Michael D., 1969–
    Oversight : representing the interests of Blacks and Latinos in Congress / Michael D.
Minta.
        p.   cm.
    Includes bibliographical references and index.
    ISBN 978-0-691-14925-7 (hardcover : alk. paper) — ISBN 978-0-691-14926-4
(pbk. : alk. paper)   1. African American legislators.   2. Hispanic American
legislators.   3. African Americans—Politics and government.   4. Hispanic Americans—
Politics and government.   5. United States. Congress.   6. Representative government
and representation—United States.   I. Title.
    JK1321.A37M56 2011
    328.73089'96073—dc22   2010052064

British Library Cataloging-in-Publication Data is available
This book has been composed in Galliard

Printed on acid-free paper.

Printed in the United States of America

10 9 8 7 6 5 4 3 2 1

To my wife, Janell Lofton-Minta

Contents

Figures and Tables

Figures

Tables

Acknowledgments

The great author and poet Langston Hughes wrote a famous poem, "Mother to Son," where a mother gives powerful motivational advice to her son. In the poem the mother tells him:

Life for me ain't been no crystal stair.
It's had tacks in it, and splinters, and boards torn up.
And places with no carpet on the floor—
Bare. But all the time I'se been a-climbin' on,
And reachin' landin's,
And turnin' corners,
And sometimes goin' in the dark . . .

Writing an academic book has been filled with some tacks and splinters along the way, but I have had many colleagues, friends, and family members who provided the invaluable support and guidance necessary to finish a project of this magnitude. Although this book has changed significantly in scope and substance from its dissertation form, I owe a debt to my former graduate school advisers, Richard Hall, Vincent Hutchings, Elisabeth Gerber, and Hanes Walton Jr. Their support and guidance were instrumental in my early growth and development as a social scientist. They allowed me to take intellectual risks and follow my own lead, even if the risks sometimes outweighed the benefits. They did not want to produce someone who did exactly what they did but someone who could find his own way and provide knowledge in areas that were not yet explored. I am glad that they were my advisers, and more important, I am glad to call them my friends.

I have met many other colleagues along the way, who have greatly assisted me in making this project better. Frank Baumgartner and Christopher Parker have provided tremendous support and feedback to me. Both have read every chapter of the book and provided detailed and insightful comments that have no doubt made this project more accessible to a broader audience than congressional scholars. In my writing, Frank pushed me to find my voice and once I did to let everyone know that I had something important to say. Chris pushed me to think about how my findings related to broader theoretical constructs that extend beyond congressional and bureaucratic politics. Claudine Gay and Katherine Tate read significant portions of the manuscript and urged me to be more precise in my claims but still make the book appealing to a general audience. I want to especially thank Princeton University Press's executive editor of political science and law, Charles Myers, for his patience, encouragement, and guidance throughout the development and writing stage of the manuscript. I have received wonderful advice on the project through conversations, meetings, or various presentations from Matt Barreto, Cristina Beltran, Barry Burden, David Canon, Daniel Carpenter, Grace Cho, Richard Fenno, Morris Fiorina, Katrina Gamble, Lisa Garcia Bedolla, Christian Grose, Kerry Haynie, Mariely Lopez-Santana, Jane Mansbridge, Benjamin Marquez, Harwood McClerking, Kristina Miler, Gary Miller, Irfan Nooruddin, Ifeoma Okwuje, Matthew Platt, Andrew Rehfeld, Beth Reingold, Lynn Sanders, Mark Sawyer, Gary Segura, Itai Sened, Charles Shipan, Gisela Sin, Valeria Sinclair-Chapman, Jae-Jae Spoon, Dara Strolovitch, and Carol Swain. I also would like to thank the Weidenbaum Center for financial support provided to this project.

I am indebted to many talented people who provided research assistance to this project. Some, such as Kim Dorazio and Brooke Thomas Allen, have worked with me for many years. Both Kim and Brooke served as managers for the data collection and coding of the congressional hearings. Words cannot express the gratitude I have for their talents and hard work. I am also grateful for the hard work and research assistance provided by Rachel Cohen, Brittany Coleman, Ashleah Gilmore, Hana Greenberg, Deborah Grohosky, Steven Marcus, Annasara Purcell, Dominick Volonnino, and Shelby Washington. Additionally, I want to thank Ruth Homrighaus for copyediting and formatting the initial draft of this manuscript and Margery Tippie for copyediting the final draft. The book is much better because of their efforts.

None of my efforts would be possible without the love and support of my immediate and extended family. My parents, David and Dorothy Johnson, have instilled in me a fierce work ethic and the good moral values that are necessary to be a good professional and person. I can never repay them for all that they have done for me. My in-laws, Spurgeon and Esther Lofton, have continued to provide love and support for my family. Trips to annual political science conferences and presentations would not have been possible without their help. This is truly amazing, considering they live in Houston and we live in St. Louis. The support, love, and encouragement of my wife, Janell Lofton-Minta, made the completion of the manuscript possible. She listened to my many ideas and read multiple iterations. When I had to work late writing or go to work-related events, Janell always picked up the slack for me. This was not an easy task, considering that she has a demanding career and is the mother of our three children, two who were born while I was completing this project. Most important, my wife and my children, Kendall, Braden, and Bryson, provide the balance between family and work that I need to be a complete person. I am truly blessed to have them in my life.

OVERSIGHT

1

Introduction

IN 2005 HURRICANE KATRINA struck the Gulf Coast region of the United States, causing major flooding and displacing many residents in Louisiana, Mississippi, and Alabama. The storm was responsible for more than a thousand deaths, most of them in Louisiana. Many people were left homeless and with no place to turn for help. Although Louisiana state and local officials, such as Governor Kathleen Blanco and Mayor Ray Nagin, received much of the blame from the national press and policymakers for not adequately responding to the disaster, the bulk of the criticism was directed toward the Federal Emergency Management Agency (FEMA). Only weeks after President George Bush had praised FEMA director Michael Brown for the agency's response to the Hurricane Katrina disaster—"Brownie, you're doing a heck of a job,"[1] he said—intense criticism by the public and by both Democrats and Republicans in Congress led to Brown's resignation.

Many members of Congress were outraged by the federal bureaucracy's ineffective and slow response to the disaster. In 2005 and 2006, Congress conducted more than 130 hearings relating to the federal response to Hurricane Katrina. Many high-ranking officials from FEMA and the Department of Homeland Security (DHS), the agency that houses FEMA, were called to testify before House and Senate committees. While FEMA's efforts were universally criticized by both Democrats and Republicans, the explanations for why the federal response was inadequate and poorly managed became fiercely partisan and racially charged. In fact, Democrats refused to participate in the hearings held by the GOP-led House Select Committee, the House committee officially charged with investigating the federal response to Hurricane Katrina, preferring instead to launch an independent investigation into the federal government's response. The Democrats most critical of the efforts of FEMA were members of the Congressional Black Caucus (CBC) and Congressional Hispanic Caucus (CHC).[2] The CBC and CHC requested that committee oversight hearings

---

[1] "A Punch Line Who Refuses to Fade Away." *The New York Times,* August 26, 2006.

[2] As a result of federal response to Hurricane Katrina, members of the CBC, CHC, and the Congressional Asian and Pacific Islander Caucus formed the Tri-Caucus to address the needs of marginalized communities. The formation of the coalitions counters conventional wisdom that minority legislators are too divided to work together on important policy issues.

be held, sponsored legislation that required FEMA to do better disaster relief planning, and testified at various congressional hearings in support of residents who could not escape the disaster. Along with failing to provide appropriate shelter, food, and water for stranded residents, minority legislators argued, FEMA had neglected to provide adequate transportation to assist in evacuating the poorest, the disabled, and elderly citizens. Black and Latino legislators, echoing the sentiments of many leaders and residents in the black and Latino communities, argued that FEMA's response would have been quicker and larger in scale if the affected residents had been white and affluent rather than black and poor. The Lower Ninth Ward, the area most affected by the breach of the levees in New Orleans, was more than 60 percent black and largely poor.

While all Democrats and Republicans were expressing their displeasure with federal relief efforts, then, black and Latino members of Congress were articulating the concerns and perspectives of groups that were largely underrepresented in congressional deliberations. Members of Congress from the Gulf Coast, such as Bennie Thompson (D-MS) and William Jefferson (D-LA), offered stinging criticism of the federal relief efforts for their constituents. In assessing under what conditions FEMA could have been more effective in responding to the disaster, Thompson said: "We need someone to run the agency who is qualified. We just can't have a political crony running an agency as important as FEMA. The other thing is that person has to have direct communication with the White House. That individual in time of an incident of national significance should not have to go through some chain of command to marshal the assets necessary to respond to that emergency. It just should not be."[3]

That legislators from Mississippi and Louisiana would advocate for their constituents is not surprising, but many minority legislators who were not from the affected areas also actively advocated for the interests of Hurricane Katrina victims. Black legislators such as Rep. Elijah Cummings (D-MD), chairman of the Congressional Black Caucus, issued harsh statements regarding the federal government response. Cummings stated in a CBC press release: "We cannot allow it to be said that the difference between those who lived and those who died in this great storm and flood of 2005 was nothing more than poverty, age or skin color."[4] There were no Latino members of Congress representing either Louisiana or Mississippi—Latinos made up less than 5 percent of the residents in New Orleans—but Latino legislators from other states provided a voice for Latino interests in the affected areas. They argued that immigrant communities along the Gulf

[3] Hearing held by Department of Homeland Security, House of Representatives: "Legislation to Strengthen FEMA and Better Integrate It into the DHS, and for Other Purposes," May 9, 2006, p. 2.
[4] CHC Press Release, 2005.

Coast were not receiving relief assistance because of language barriers.[5] In addition to not receiving access to services, these legislators argued, Latino citizens and immigrants were being intimidated and harassed by relief workers and US Marshals. Rep. Raul Grijalva (D-AZ) stated: "Every victim is a victim. To pick out one victim and allow them to suffer greater consequences is not only appalling, it is inhumane." [6]

The aftermath of Hurricane Katrina serves as a stark reminder of how federal actions by agencies such as FEMA and DHS can profoundly affect the lives of Americans, as well as of the important role that Congress plays in holding these agencies accountable for their actions. The congressional oversight by minority legislators witnessed in the wake of Katrina also draws attention to important questions about the nature of congressional representation. In 2009, more than four years after Hurricane Katrina devastated Louisiana and Mississippi and long after the media spotlight had moved off the Gulf Coast, black and Latino members of Congress continue to actively devote their scarce time and resources to advocating on behalf of citizens who do not reside in their districts. Legislators who are not from the Gulf Coast states, such as Nydia Velazquez and Elijah Cummings, still show up at oversight hearings and make comments directing FEMA officials to devote more resources toward mostly class-based policies, such as affordable housing and community development, that are designed to improve the lives of poor and minority residents affected by the Hurricane Katrina disaster. What factors motivate these legislators to keep an eye on federal agencies in the absence of media attention?

The answer to this question is linked to debates about the nature of congressional representation that are older than the Constitution itself. The Constitution's proponents (the Federalists), such as James Madison and Alexander Hamilton, argued that what is today called "descriptive representation"—in which the members of Congress resemble the groups present in society—is not essential for Congress to adequately represent the people. Though the concept of descriptive representation presumes that a group's interests will be best served by a legislator from that group, the Federalists argued that this is not the case, as constituents can always use elections to remove legislators who do not represent their interests (Rossiter 1961). To borrow Madison's example, one does not have to be a farmer to represent the interests of farmers in one's district.

More than two hundred years later, political theorists and researchers continue to debate whether descriptive representatives are necessary to provide adequate representation of constituent interests in Congress. Studies of congressional activity, most of which focus on legislators' voting

[5]CHC Press Release, 2005.
[6]CHC Press Release, 2005.

records, have not only failed to settle the question, they have also raised new questions, both methodological and substantive. Congressional scholars studying race and ethnicity, as well as liberal and conservative critics of descriptive representation, have generally sided with the argument that one does not have to descriptively represent the group in order to represent the interests of the group (Cameron, Epstein, and O'Halloran 1996; Guinier 1995; Hero and Tolbert 1995; Swain 1993; Thernstrom 1987). Other scholars have found, however, that race and ethnicity play a significant role in determining legislators' support for minority-interest issues (Canon 1999; Lublin 1997; Tate 2003; Welch and Hibbing 1984; Whitby 1997). Similarly, scholars examining the impact of gender and representation have come to similar conclusions, finding that female legislators are more likely than male legislators to advocate for and provide a voice to issues that traditionally are of concern to women (Bratton and Haynie 1999; Kathlene 1994; Reingold 2000; Swers 1998, 2002). A number of scholars have pointed to the inadequacy of voting records to measure the extent to which racial and ethnic minorities in Congress succeed in representing their constituents, prompting a search for better methods. Contrary to the critics of descriptive representation, these scholars have found that race and ethnicity provides a voice to underrepresented minorities in areas beyond roll-call voting (Canon 1999; Casellas 2011; Gamble 2007; Griffin and Newman 2008; Grose 2011; Haynie 2001; Minta 2009; Sinclair-Chapman 2003; Tate 2003). Examining forms of legislative activity other than voting permits investigation of this new line and growing body of research on political representation and race and ethnic politics, suggesting answers to an important question: Do minority representatives offer something to their minority constituents that white representatives of identical political orientation do not? That is, would a white legislator who votes identically to a black or Latino legislator necessarily represent his or her district's blacks and Latinos just as well?

This study demonstrates via an analysis of congressional oversight activities that descriptive representatives—in this case, black and Latino legislators—provide superior substantive representation of minority interests. Investigating what I refer to as "legislative intervention" in committee oversight activities shifts the focus beyond assessing whether legislators are voting the "right way," or in the manner their constituents prefer, to examining how much time and effort they spend intervening in agency policymaking on behalf of their constituents. This approach, unlike one that relies on roll-call voting records, enables me to measure the intensity of legislators' interest in certain policies. After all, legislators have limited time and resources, and their decision to direct their attention to engaging in oversight speaks volumes about the level of their commitment to an issue, particularly because most oversight—in marked contrast to the example of the congressional deliberations regarding Hurricane Katrina—fails to capture the attention of the national media and the American public and consequently is unlikely to improve any given legislator's odds of reelection.

While most legislators are reluctant to engage in the workhorse activity of oversight, I find that black and Latino legislators believe they must take action to collectively uplift blacks and Latinos, respectively. I argue that an ideology of "strategic group uplift" explains the difference in advocacy efforts, or interventions, between minority and white legislators. The presence of blacks and Latinos in Congress leads to qualitatively better representation of black and Latino interests by providing a voice and perspective to underrepresented and marginalized communities that are not normally included in the public policy-making process.

As the chapters that follow will show, black and Latino legislators are more responsive to the interests of blacks, Latinos, and the poor than are white legislators. They are more likely to advocate on issues such as racial profiling and affirmative action. They are also more likely to intervene in agency decision making by attending, testifying, and engaging in deliberations at congressional oversight hearings in support of minority interests. Moreover, minority legislators write more letters urging agency officials to pursue the enforcement of civil rights policies, and they also spend significant time and effort promoting and advocating for class-based solutions that benefit all racial and ethnic groups, such as efforts to end poverty and increase Medicaid and community development funding.

Not only do black and Latino legislators engage more in oversight activity, but their presence in the committee room increases the chances that black and Latino perspectives and concerns will be addressed and included in committee deliberations. Black and Latino legislators bring a distinct perspective to policy deliberations that white legislators do not provide. They are effective at countering negative stereotypes about minorities in policy debates relating to issues such as affirmative action and affordable housing. As one might expect, the impact of race and ethnicity is more pronounced in policy debates relating to racial and ethnic issues, such as racial profiling and bilingual education. The impact of racial and ethnic background is not limited to racial or ethnic issues, however; it also informs policy debates on social welfare issues, such as welfare reform.

Voting as a Measure of Representation

Though the conclusions outlined above may seem commonsensical, a number of contemporary scholars are skeptical about the degree to which descriptive characteristics matter in terms of providing representation to constituents (Pennock 1979; Pitkin 1967). They argue that the logic of descriptive representation fails in two critical respects: First, the requirement that a legislature resemble the diversity of groups present in society, such as farmers, businesspeople, or racial or ethnic minorities, has very little to do with how policies that substantively affect members of that society are produced (Pitkin 1967). According to Pitkin, legislators should be judged on their actions, not just their closeness in characteristics to their constituents: "The activity of representing as acting for others must be defined in terms of what the representative does and how he does it, or in some combination of these two considerations" (143). In this view, providing substantive representation requires mainly the casting of the "right" votes on policies by reflecting constituent opinions. When applying this concept to racial or ethnic representation, we can see that one does not have to be a Latino legislator, for instance, to vote in favor of a bill that prohibits discrimination against Latino constituents.

Pitkin's argument is illuminated by recent research into the consequences of racial gerrymandering, or the process by which states draw congressional districts in order to increase the likelihood that racial minorities can successfully elect candidates of their same racial or ethnic background. Historically, black and Latino candidates for Congress and other minorities have been underrepresented in Congress compared to their demographic makeup in society. In the 110th Congress (2007–2009), for example, black legislators represented 9 percent, or 42, of the 440 members in the House, which is less than the 12 percent that blacks constitute in the U.S population.[7] Latino legislators represented 6 percent of the members, which is less than the 14 percent that Latinos constitute in the US population. Much of the underrepresentation is based on the fact that in majority-white districts, whites have been reluctant to vote for black candidates (Reeves 1997). For example, Canon (1999) found that, in 6,667 House elections in white-majority districts between 1966 and 1996, blacks only won 35, or 0.52 percent, of these elections.

In an attempt to get more blacks and Latinos in Congress, in the early 1990s many black and Latino leaders urged the creation of majority-black and majority-Latino districts. These leaders believed that the creation of these districts would increase the electoral chances of black and Latino candidates, with the likely result of increasing minority representation in Congress. Proponents of the creation of majority-black districts, such as the Congressional Black Caucus and minority interest groups, believed that

[7]There are 435 members in the House of Representatives, along with delegates from American Samoa, the District of Columbia, Guam, and the Virgin Islands and a resident commissioner of Puerto Rico. Information on demographics in Congress obtained from CRS Report for Congress, RS 22007, Membership of the 110th Congress: A Profile. Information on voting-age population obtained from 2004 General Demographic Characteristics: 2004, Data Set: 2004 American Community Survey.

not only would more blacks be elected to Congress, but black legislators would make a difference in the quality of representation on issues that blacks tend to support. Opponents of racial gerrymandering argued that these newly constructed districts were unconstitutional and that the race of the member does not make a difference in the quality of representation provided to blacks. As a result of racial redistricting, the number of black representatives in Congress increased, with blacks being elected in southern states such as South Carolina, North Carolina, Alabama, and Louisiana for the first time since Reconstruction.

Investigations of whether this increase in descriptive representation represents a positive step for black Americans have produced mixed results. Swain (1993) argued that majority-minority districts were not necessary for black candidates to get elected to Congress or for black constituents to receive fair and adequate representation of their interests. Relying mainly on roll-call voting scores, she found no difference between the voting of black and white representatives on general minority-interest issues, such as civil rights and social welfare issues. As a result, she concluded that descriptive representation did not lead to more legislation being passed that was favorable to minorities. Furthermore, after interviewing both black and white members of Congress, she found that white Democratic legislators were more effective at representing black interests than were black Democratic legislators. Swain points out that although concentrating black voters into minority districts increased the number of black representatives in Congress, it led to more Republicans being elected as well. Because Republicans were more hostile to black interests than were Democrats, she argued, blacks would be better served by electing Democrats, regardless of their race.

Cameron, Epstein, and O'Halloran (1996) examined whether majority-minority districts maximize substantive black representation in Congress. Like Swain (1993), they found that white legislators in the North had similar voting records on minority interests as black legislators. Thus, they argued that creating majority-minority districts in the North did not maximize substantive representation, because it removed minorities from marginal districts and hurt Democrats' chances of being elected. In the South, however, they found that to maximize black representation, districts should be constructed that are at least 47 percent black (Cameron, Epstein, and O'Halloran 1996). Differing from Swain, then, they concluded that descriptive representation is most important in southern states.

Taken together, these two studies of black representation suggest that the creation of majority-minority districts successfully increases the number of black legislators elected to Congress, but that increased descriptive representation can result in less effective substantive representation of minority interests—what Lublin (1999) refers to as the "paradox of representation."

Research into descriptive representation by Latinos has produced equally mixed results. Hero and Tolbert (1995) have found that having Latino representatives in Congress does little to improve the substantive representation of minority interests. Other studies, by contrast, show that having Latino representatives plays an important role in providing substantive representation to Latino interests (Casellas 2009; Welch and Hibbing 1984).

While assessments of congressional voting provide valuable insight into the effect of race or ethnicity in this important legislative arena, one shortcoming of such studies is that they may overstate the degree of partisan unity among legislators on minority-interest issues. For example, when the Democrats control the House, Hall and Heflin (1994) argue, differences are not readily apparent between black and white legislators in the Democratic Party because controversial racial issues are censored before they come to the House floor for a vote. Hall and Heflin note that party leaders do not want to show a split in the party, so the only bills that come up for a vote are the ones on which most white and black Democrats agree. This may be especially true in a Republican-majority Congress; as the modal legislation moves further to the right, more agreement should exist between moderate and liberal Democrats in opposition to the legislation (Cox and McCubbins 2005; Lawrence, Maltzman, and Smith 2006). As a result, white legislators appear as though they are more in step with minority legislators and minority constituents than they actually are.

In addition, many scholars find that as an indicator of black policy preferences, the roll-call voting indicators used to assess substantive representation, such as Leadership Conference on Civil Rights scores, include a host of issues that either blacks do not care about or on which their views are not different from those of whites (Hutchings 1998; Swain 1993; Whitby 1997). The 2001–2002 version of the Leadership Conference on Civil Rights voting score index, for example, included tax reform, an issue on which, according to most public opinion surveys, blacks usually do not differ dramatically from whites. Thus, when trying to evaluate whether legislators provide substantive representation to blacks, this measure is unlikely to find differences between black and white legislators.

Another limitation of existing studies of political representation that use roll-call data is that scholars rarely examine whether black and Latino legislators are just as active on class-based policies that address the poor as they are on racial/ethnic policies. Instead, these studies usually conflate racial/ethnic issues with social welfare issues, thus overstating the extent to which a member's race or ethnicity may motivate him or her to address the interests of lower-income minorities and the poor. It is important to separate class-based policies from racial/ethnic issues, because normative theorists question whether one can assume that descriptive representatives can effectively represent the interests of all groups (Dovi 2002; Phillips 1995; Young 2000). Many studies pertaining to the intersection of race, class, and gender show that the shared experiences of minority legislators do not necessarily extend to enabling them to provide adequate representation to the diverse interests of all members within their racial or ethnic group (Cohen 1999; Hancock 2004; Strolovitch 2007). Cohen (1999), for example, found that the CBC, while claiming to represent the interests of all blacks, failed to actively advocate for measures to combat the spread of HIV/AIDS among black gays and lesbians and intravenous drug users.

Given the limitations of roll-call voting studies, it is important in gauging the necessity and effectiveness of descriptive representation to look beyond voting to other forms of legislative behavior, such as engaging in deliberations, which are excluded from Pitkin's concept of substantive representation. Like other scholars, I argue that Pitkin's definition of substantive representation is too narrow and creates an unnecessary separation between voting and policy debates surrounding the passage and implementation of legislation, which can be just as important. A number of studies have considered the effect of descriptive representation in less constrained legislative activities, which are unlikely to reflect the strong censoring influence of political parties. For example, Canon (1999) examined the effect of race on legislative participation in activities such as floor speeches, employment of district staff, and sponsorship of race-related bills. He found that white legislators were less likely than black legislators to introduce or cosponsor racial or partly racial bills, to address racial issues in House floor speeches, or to mention race-related matters in newsletters to their constituents. Similarly, other scholars have found that black legislators are more likely than white legislators to sponsor and cosponsor race-related bills (Bratton and Haynie 1999; Canon 1999; Haynie 2001; Sinclair-Chapman 2003; Tate 2003), participate in mark-up hearings (Gamble 2007), discuss racial themes in floor speeches, and hire racially diverse district staff (Canon 1999).

As the oversight activities following Hurricane Katrina suggest, another area in which members of Congress do important work of representation is the oversight of federal agency policymaking. Indeed, congressional oversight of federal agencies responds directly to Pitkin's (1967) charge that descriptive representation must be related to governance for it to be substantive and meaningful. Yet congressional oversight seldom receives attention in studies of the substantive representation of minority interests. With the exception of the work of Hall (1996) and Gamble (2007), little research has been devoted to examining to what extent race and ethnicity influence how actively legislators advocate for the interests of minority constituents in committee activities. As a result, we do not yet have a complete view of the representative activities of legislators.

Oversight as a Form of Political Representation

FEMA's failure to adequately respond to Hurricane Katrina confirms the fears of many scholars and observers of politics that federal agencies do not always follow the wishes of Congress and the people (Bibby 1968; Ogul 1976). Although Congress delegates much of the enforcement of laws to the federal bureaucracy, constituents rely on legislators to ensure that federal agencies enforce and implement these laws (see, for example, Carpenter 2001; Epstein and O'Halloran 1999; Huber 2007; Huber and Shipan 2002; Mayhew 1991; McCubbins and Schwartz 1984; Weingast and Moran 1983). The protection of racial or ethnic minorities, in particular, has depended heavily on the willingness of Congress to vigorously oversee the federal executive agencies that implement laws protecting civil rights and social welfare. Measuring the extent to which Congress, the branch that is closest to the people, provides an adequate check on the federal bureaucracy is a concern of many democratic theorists.

Participation in deliberations and the correspondence that legislators send to agency policymakers form an important part of substantive representation that is largely ignored in the extant literature. Yet deliberations in the legislative assembly are an important part of governing. Before legislators can make a decision on whether to vote for or against a law or before an agency can implement a policy, deliberations must be held in Congress. Legislators' interventions allow legislators to convey their constituents' preferences or their own preferences to agency bureaucrats regarding agency efforts to implement a federal law or program.

To ensure that agencies follow the will of Congress, congressional committees can initiate hearings and investigate agency policymaking and implementation (Bibby 1968; Ogul 1976; Aberbach 1990). Investigations and hearings are typically used to uncover wrongdoing and misconduct by federal officials, but hearings also provide legislators with an update on the activities and operations of federal agencies. Although hearings and investigations are the most popular approach to oversight, legislators can take a more passive approach, which frees them from constant, time-consuming monitoring. They do this by installing a variety of administrative controls that place the burden on interest groups to notify Congress or sound what McCubbins and Schwartz (1984) refer to as "fire alarms." Congress can also effectively limit potential wrongdoing by agencies by crafting legislation that limits agencies' discretion in implementing public policy (Epstein and O'Halloran 1999; Huber and Shipan 2002; McCubbins, Noll and Weingast 1987).

During committee deliberations, individual legislators can request either verbally or in writing that federal agencies dedicate more resources to agency enforcement efforts. They can also be critical of the inaction of agency officials in response to previous congressional requests to replace or remove agency personnel. In a hearing focusing on efforts by the US Department of Housing and Urban Development (HUD) to enforce fair housing laws, Congresswoman Nydia Velazquez (D-NY) expressed dissatisfaction at the inability of the Bush administration to find a replacement to head the Civil Rights Section of HUD: "Eighteen months into the President's term, the position of Assistant Secretary for Housing—for Fair Housing and Equal Opportunity—remains unfilled. In fact, the current nominee, Ms. Carolyn Peoples, was only submitted by the President in May. Furthermore, she has had very limited experience administering fair housing laws. I take this to be a troubling indication of the low level of importance placed on these issues by the administration, one that I hope will soon be reviewed. This void has left us with a backlog of fair housing complaints that members of our communities tell us take far longer than the statutorily required deadline of 100 days to address."

Although legislators can intervene positively on behalf of minority interests, some legislators defend the status quo or do not want an increased effort by an agency. In the same HUD oversight committee hearing, for example, Congressman Gary Miller (R-CA) defended the Bush administration's efforts to implement antidiscrimination laws: "I am very pleased that we are having this hearing. I think some things might be blown out of perspective. I have to agree there has been lack of enforcement on certain programs and policies, and especially when it comes to disabled and minorities in the past. But I think that is somewhat in the past. I think the new administration [Bush administration] is making every attempt to remove the problems that we faced in the past. So I do not know if it is necessarily a problem that requires new legislation."

Using legislators' interventions to evaluate their substantive representation of constituent interests provides advantages over studying roll-call voting. First, this approach is more precise, because it goes beyond simply reporting whether or not legislators are voting in accordance with their constituents' interests to measure how much time and effort legislators spend advocating for issues on behalf of their constituents. Considering interventions permits a distinction to be made, for example, between a member of Congress who spends fifty hours researching and dedicating staff resources to advocate for a measure favoring civil rights and a legislator who supports civil rights but dedicates only two hours to advocating for stronger enforcement in committee deliberations.

It is useful to measure congressional activities that are costly in terms of time, moreover, because in participating in such activities, legislators demonstrate

intensity of commitment. Legislators have many issues vying for their attention but are limited in time and resources that they have to devote to
them (Hall and Miler 2000). Hall and Miler explain what attendance at a
hearing entails: "The legislator must fashion a response to an agency
whose principal advantage is its expertise and whose presumptive authority
is a preexisting statute. At a minimum, the legislator's staff would need to
spend time acquiring and digesting information about the agency proposal; analyzing its consequences for the member's constituents; formulat-
ing and justifying points of criticism (or endorsement); and then preparing
the legislator to participate in the dialogue that might ensue" (4). Thus,
the decision by a legislator to attend an oversight hearing and engage in
deliberations is not a costless one, nor is such attendance a purely symbolic
gesture. Rather, a legislator's decision to commit resources to oversight
speaks to that member's intensity of commitment for or against the policy
issue under consideration. In considering legislators' interventions, moreover, we can move beyond Hall's (1996) measure of how active legislators
are in committee deliberations to indicate as well whether these legislators
are for or against a given policy. This approach permits us to gauge if legislators' actions are consistent with the opinions of blacks and Latinos.

Not only does the decision to intervene in agency policymaking require
a heavy investment of legislators' scarce resources and time, it also offers
little in the way of electoral rewards (Aberbach 1990; Arnold 1990; Hall
and Miler 2000; McCubbins and Schwartz 1984). Unlike roll-call voting
records, which usually are more visible and are followed closely by constituents and potential election opponents, most oversight occurs out of
the purview of constituents and competitors. Consequently, individual
legislators' involvement in oversight activities (or lack thereof) may not be
easily traced back to them (Arnold 1990). Because the benefits of such
activities may be broad, constituents will likely not be able to attribute
these benefits to the efforts of their individual representative, nor can that
representative successfully claim credit for his or her actions (Arnold 1990;
Hall and Miler 2000; McCubbins and Schwartz 1984). Legislators' interventions in oversight activities are therefore more likely than their votes to
reveal their true positions and less likely to reflect the influence of party or
reelection pressure.

Strategic Group Uplift

The conventional wisdom of political theorists is that legislators' actions
are motivated primarily by strategic factors related to reelection and constituency influence (e.g., Fiorina 1974; Mayhew 1974). To understand why
black and Latino legislators devote more time and energy to the "work-

horse" activities of oversight than do their white peers, it is necessary to look beyond strategy to the influence of race. I argue that most black and Latino legislators, unlike most white legislators, believe that not only must they represent their constituents, but they have an extra obligation to represent the interests of blacks and Latinos nationally and internationally— to uplift their racial or ethnic group. Evidence of this conviction can be found, among other places, in the Congressional Black Caucus and Congressional Hispanic Caucus, which exist as a result of minority legislators' commitment to engage in collective action that furthers the interests of blacks and Latinos, respectively. The degree to which black and Latino legislators can engage in the advocacy of minority interests in Congress is limited temporally and by resources, by the interests of their political party, and by the practical consideration that they must engage in activities to ensure their reelection to office. These limitations require that legislators be strategic about the ways in which they work on behalf of minorities. Thus, I refer to the ideology that motivates black and Latino legislators to monitor federal agencies' activities and ensure responsiveness to constituencies as one of "strategic group uplift."

The concept of strategic group uplift is grounded in survey research and normative political theory relating to the idea of shared racial and ethnic group consciousness, which I explore in some detail in chapter 2. Survey research on the general public shows that the majority of blacks, regardless of their socioeconomic status, believe that what happens to African Americans as a group also affects them individually (Dawson 1994; Gurin, Hatchett, and Jackson 1989). This research finds that black people who possess racial group consciousness and a perception that their fates are linked to those of other black people are more likely to favor race-based programs and social welfare programs than are whites (Conover 1984; Miller, Gurin, Gurin, and Malanchuk 1981; Tate 1993). Although blacks and Latinos are far from monolithic groups, on political issues such as race or ethnicity, strategic group uplift motivates minority legislators to transcend intragroup differences based on income, class, and, with Latinos, differences among subnational groups.

Normative theorists argue that shared group experiences also play a significant role influencing the activities of political institutions such as Congress. They argue that because underrepresented groups share the experience of having been discriminated against because of their race or ethnicity, racial or ethnic minorities are more likely to represent the interests of marginalized groups in the public policy-making process (Williams 1998; Young 2000). As a result of their shared experiences, blacks and Latinos bring different viewpoints and understandings of the causes of problems and conflicts in society, as well as the possible effects of proposed solutions (Mansbridge 1999; Young 2000). Their unique perspective is crucial in a political context in which members of these marginalized groups have been excluded from political discussion and the policy-making process in Congress.

The concept of strategic group uplift interacts with existing accounts of congressional behavior that emphasize how the desire for reelection and direct constituent pressure motivate legislators. Black and Latino members of Congress feel these pressures, too, of course; the concept of strategic group uplift suggests that these motivations interact with the key third motivation of racial and ethnic group consciousness to guide minority legislators' actions. Understanding the relationship between these concepts provides a more complete picture of the political representation of constituent interests and suggests how shared experiences play an important role in the delivery of substantive representation to minority constituents.

The ideology of strategic group uplift not only benefits minorities, moreover, but also the nation as a whole by bringing a diversity of opinions and perspectives to legislative hearings. Normative political theorists argue that diversity of experience in committee deliberations leads to better public policymaking (Mansbridge 1999; Williams 1998; Young 2000). Young writes that "special representation of marginalized social groups" brings "situated knowledges" to bear on "political discussion and decision-making." She explains: "Because of their social positioning, members of structurally differentiated groups often have different understandings of the causes of the problems and conflicts and the possible effects of proposed solutions. They have differing perceptions of one another and different understandings of the society's history and current relationships. If only a few of those understandings influence discussion and decision-making, political actors are more likely to perpetuate injustice or take imprudent actions" (2000, 145). When disadvantaged groups are provided a voice, their perspectives are injected in congressional deliberations in ways that even the most liberal white supporters could not articulate. This is not to imply the essentialist argument that only blacks can represent blacks or only Latinos can represent Latino interests; however, these legislators bring to bear backgrounds and collective group experiences that they could have obtained only by being a member of the group.

Chapter Outline

The chapters that follow present this argument in greater detail. The first two chapters offer some theoretical and historical background. Chapter 2 outlines the relationship between race, ethnicity, and substantive representation via an in-depth discussion of how racial and ethnic group consciousness operates among black and Latino representatives in Congress. The chapter that follows examines the history of the federal government's role in securing and denying civil rights protections and social welfare benefits to blacks and Latinos. This discussion highlights the extent to which Congress relies on minority members to engage in oversight as a way to secure these protections and benefits for minorities across the nation.

Chapters 4 and 5 analyze more than three thousand pages of congressional oversight hearings transcripts from the 103rd Congress (1993–1995), 104th Congress (1995–1997), and 107th Congress (2001–2003) to demonstrate that black and Latino legislators advocate more than white legislators in minority-interest congressional oversight hearings. I find that black legislators invest the most time, energy, and resources in ensuring that bureaucracies implement civil rights and social welfare policies, followed by Latinos. Chapter 4 focuses on civil rights advocacy, while chapter 5 investigates social welfare interventions. In addition to examining how much time legislators spend advocating for minority interests, I analyze the interactions between legislators and witnesses at the oversight hearings, particularly exchanges between officials of the bureaucracy and legislators. I consider the content of interventions by members and whether they support or oppose the policy under question. These chapters also examine the content of legislators' questions and the frequency of their comments.

The final chapter discusses the overall findings of this project and its implications for minority representation in the US Congress, and it suggests paths for further research. Generally, communities with lower levels of education and income are less likely to participate in politics (Verba and Nie 1972; Verba, Schlotzman, and Brady 1995). Even though blacks vote more than do whites, they are generally less active in other forms of political activity. Descriptive characteristics such as race or ethnicity can play an instrumental role in enhancing legislators' responsiveness to minority constituents in ways that strategic factors alone do not explain. The implication is that minority communities rely disproportionately on the actions of descriptive representatives to provide a voice for them.

2

Race, Ethnicity, and a Theory of Substantive Representation in Congressional Oversight

IN THE EARLY 1990s, black farm groups wanted the US Department of Agriculture (USDA) to implement a court consent decree that required the agency to compensate black farmers for the department's role in discriminating against black farmers in the farm lending program. Legislators and Sanford Bishop (D-GA) advocated for black farmers. Also included among those advocates was John Conyers (D-MI). Speaking out for the interests of black farmers was not a new role for Conyers, who has spent more than twenty years as a vocal critic of discrimination in the USDA's farm loan program. Conyers has requested that committee oversight hearings be held, sponsored legislation that required the USDA to comply with the provisions of the consent decree, and testified at various congressional hearings in support of farmers. What is unusual about Conyers's interventions is that he represents an urban district that includes the city of Detroit and has no identifiable agricultural interest. Why would a legislator from Detroit actively devote his scarce time and resources to advocating for black farmers?

Accounts that rely mainly on legislators' strategic calculations cannot adequately explain why a legislator like Conyers decides to advocate on behalf of individuals who are not in his district (Fiorina 1974; Kingdon 1989; Mayhew 1974). Nor do strategic explanations account for why minority and white members on the same congressional committees with similar district interests differ in their level of advocacy for minority interests in oversight hearings. This chapter develops a theory of why black and Latino legislators choose to intervene in congressional oversight hearings on behalf of other blacks and Latinos when most of their constituents and likely political challengers are not necessarily paying attention. I argue in this book that an ideology of what I call "strategic group uplift" plays a prominent role in motivating legislators to actively engage in committee oversight. According to this theory, black and Latino legislators' advocacy efforts for minority interests are motivated simultaneously by their desire to be reelected and by their goal of improving the socioeconomic and political status of fellow blacks and Latinos. Embedded in the concept of strategic group uplift is the idea that black and Latino legislators commit to representing the interests of all black and Latinos, respectively, even those individuals who are not in their district. Minority legislators must learn to balance their desire for reelection against their desire to uplift fellow members of their race/ethnicity. White legislators usually do not face this challenge; thus, strategic group uplift motivates African American and Latino members of Congress to intervene in agency policymaking in different ways than white legislators. The extent to which strategic group uplift motivates legislators may vary by policy dimension (racial versus nonracial policy) and the degree of partisan control of government (unified versus divided government).

The "strategic" element of the concept of "strategic group uplift" acknowledges the primary importance of reelection among legislators' goals. Legislators structure their efforts in Congress around activities that increase their odds of reelection (Fiorina 1974; Mayhew 1974). They must engage in activities that demonstrate to their constituents that they are being responsive to their interests. For instance, legislators from rural areas with agriculture interests select to serve on committees that have jurisdiction over agriculture issues, such as the House Agriculture Committee, which provides them with opportunities to ensure that their constituents receive an appropriate level of goods and resources (Weingast and Marshall 1989). A legislator who serves on the House Agriculture Committee can ensure that his constituents are receiving their fair share of, say, the peanut subsidies that are contained within the Farm Bill.

Not only must legislators engage in activities that benefit their districts, they must also ensure that their constituents are aware that they are being responsive to their needs. This consideration motivates them to engage in activities that are likely to be visible to their constituents and for which they can successfully claim credit (Mayhew 1974). As a result, legislators devote much attention to roll-call voting, because they know that constituents pay attention to roll-call voting records during electoral contests. Roll-call votes are highly visible, and legislators whose records indicate that they are out of touch with their constituents' interests in a given Congress are more likely to be challenged in the next election than those legislators who vote in accordance with their constituents' interests. By contrast, legislators have few opportunities to claim credit among their constituents for engaging in oversight.

While all members of Congress face the pressure of making the right decisions to increase their chances at reelection, black and Latino legislators, unlike most white legislators, face an additional pressure: they are motivated by a group norm that requires them to engage in collective group action on issues of concern to other blacks and Latinos. White legislators are mainly responsible for being responsive to the constituents in their districts, whereas black and Latino legislators are also expected to represent the interests of all blacks and Latinos nationally. The strategy they pursue of "strategic group uplift" falls at the intersection of their electoral goals and their commitment to advance group interests. The rest of the chapter explores the origins and presence of this concept in the black and Latino community and among members of Congress and uses it to generate hypotheses regarding congressional oversight behavior.

Origins and Presence of Strategic Group Uplift in African Americans

W. E. B. Du Bois argued that blacks who are highly educated and skilled have a responsibility to help improve the status of other blacks throughout the country (Du Bois 1903). This argument suggests that black Americans share a common fate and that the life chances of individual blacks are determined by the collective well-being of blacks as a group. A history of slavery and oppression, racial discrimination, and the fight for civil rights are responsible for instilling in black Americans strong feelings of group attachment (Dawson 1994; Gurin, Hatchett and Jackson 1989; Tate 1993). Scholars have also suggested that common fate perceptions developed as a result of socialization and other life experiences at the individual level and that these experiences and perceptions are reinforced by other individual experiences (McClerking 2001). Black Americans with a strong sense of "racial group consciousness" can be expected not only to identify with and feel connected to other blacks but also to engage in collective action that advances the group's interests. Using responses obtained from a national survey of black attitudes, researchers have demonstrated the existence of a sense of "linked fate," or common fate, as well as of racial group consciousness among ordinary black citizens. They find that many blacks believe that what happens to the group also affects them individually (Dawson 1994; Gurin, Hatchett, and Jackson 1989; Tate 1993). Dawson (1994) goes further and argues that many black Americans do not separate the group interest from their individual self-interest.

Perceptions of sharing a common fate play a vital role in shaping how blacks evaluate policies and determine which political candidates to support. For example, scholars have found that blacks who possessed common fate perceptions were more likely to vote for Jesse Jackson in the 1984 and 1988 presidential runs than those who did not (Dawson 1994; Tate 1993). In addition to supporting black presidential candidates, blacks with common fate perceptions were more likely to back racial and social welfare programs. Specifically, the possession of common fate perceptions had a strong liberalizing effect on black policy preferences. Blacks who were strong race identifiers were more likely to support guaranteed jobs, a minimum standard of living, and increased governmental spending on social welfare programs, such as jobs for the unemployed and food stamps (Tate 1993). Strong race identifiers were also easier to recruit, mobilize, and organize for political participation. Moreover, these studies found that the majority of blacks shared common fate perceptions regardless of their socioeconomic status; however, those who were highly educated and possessed more income were more likely to have common fate perceptions (Dawson 1994; Gurin, Hatchett, and Jackson 1989). This finding is consistent with Du Bois's belief that black elites have a responsibility to improve the socioeconomic and political conditions of other blacks.

Studies strongly suggest the existence of common fate perceptions and racial group consciousness among members of Congress (Fenno 2003; Swain 1993). Testimony given by a black representative at a hearing before the House Committee on Government Reform pertaining to racial and ethnic profiling provides anecdotal evidence of this commitment. In the hearing, Rep. Elijah Cummings (D-MD) identified with African American males as a group and mentioned the challenges that he and other black men face when they encounter law enforcement officials:

> It's so interesting when we talk about the perceptions of how some white people look at racial profiling and maybe African Americans or Hispanics may look at it. But, you know, as an African-American man, I can tell you that you begin to live your life with an extra bit of caution. I mean, you talk to most black men, they will tell you that they make sure that their lights are fixed on their cars, they make sure that no tags are hanging down, they make sure that everything is in place, because they don't want to be stopped and because we're afraid of what's going to happen. (*The Benefits of Audio-Visual Technology in Addressing Racial Profiling*, 108)

Cummings not only identifies with African Americans but also engages in collective action that furthers the interests of the group. He spends significant time at oversight hearings supporting federal legislation that would require states to keep statistics on traffic stops of individuals by race and ethnicity. He was also responsible for requesting the oversight hearing on racial profiling, which he called a "menacing problem."

The research on common fate perceptions finds that blacks who were involved in the civil rights movement are particularly likely to possess a sense of linked fate with other blacks. In the same hearing, Rep. Eleanor Holmes Norton (D-DC) testified about the impact that the civil rights movement had on her and its relationship to her views on racial profiling: "I come out of the civil rights movement, where if I got on a train from New York to Washington, I sat anywhere I wanted to. I'm a fourth-generation Washingtonian. If I went to see my grandfather in North Carolina, I had to change my seat. I thought we were long past—we bow to

States' rights in this place, but I thought we were long past the point where we would make anybody's human rights contingent upon the state that person happened to be in" (*The Benefits of Audio-Visual Technology in Addressing Racial Profiling*, 115).

Black legislators are expected by the black community as well as by their colleagues to advocate for the interests of blacks in their districts *and* for the interests of blacks nationwide—to perform what Mansbridge (2003) refers to as "surrogate representation." In interviews with Rep. Stephanie Tubbs Jones (D-OH), political scientist Richard Fenno (2003) found that Tubbs Jones did not initially view herself as a representative of constituents beyond her district, but she soon realized that many black legislators looked to her to address issues that came up throughout the state. Congressional Black Caucus members expected Tubbs Jones, a Democrat from Cleveland, to become involved in mediating a racial conflict in Cincinnati related to a police shooting of a black man during a traffic stop, for example. Even though Cincinnati was not in her district, another CBC member who wanted to get involved showed deference to Tubbs Jones because she was from Ohio. As a result of this episode, Tubbs Jones began to realize that her constituency extended beyond her district: "I had already learned that because I am the only black member of Congress from Ohio that I can be helpful to people outside my district. Many black people call on me for help because I understand their situation. When I first came to Congress, I didn't realize that people outside my district would look to me for help and that I could be helpful" (Fenno 2003, 247). Focusing on the problem in Cincinnati did little to advance her electoral goals and may have diverted her attention from issues of concern to her constituents in the Cleveland area. However, Tubbs Jones was expected to engage in "surrogate representation" because she was the only black legislator in Ohio.

Swain (1993) found that black legislators had a much broader perception of who encompassed their constituency than did white legislators. The black legislators she studied felt they had a commitment to represent the interests of not just blacks in their districts, but of all blacks nationally and internationally, as well as disadvantaged people. Writing about congressman Mickey Leland (D-TX), who chaired the Congressional Black Caucus, she noted, "Before Leland's death, his district administrator told me: What people don't understand is that Mickey Leland must be the congressman for the entire Southwest. There isn't another black congressman in this general vicinity, unless you go to the Deep South or the Midwest" (218).

The Congressional Black Caucus plays a role in reinforcing the collective group uplift philosophy. Founded in 1971, the stated purpose of the CBC is to serve the interests of all blacks in the country. All members of the CBC are black Democrats. According to its founders, the CBC provides a forum to address issues that the Democratic Party would not address normally (Clay 1993). Through weekly meetings and discussions of legislation that may have an impact on black constituents, CBC members are reminded of the importance of supporting policies that help advance the collective group interests of blacks and not just their own constituents.

In addition to the Congressional Black Caucus, black legislators are members of many political and social organizations that serve to reinforce their group consciousness (Dawson 1994; Gurin, Hatchett, and Jackson 1989; Tate 1993). These organizations not only remind legislators that their individual life chances are tied to those of other blacks but also encourage them to take collective action that will promote the interests of the group as a whole. Many predominantly black churches and political, fraternal, and business organizations were created partly as a result of the racial discrimination that excluded blacks from predominately white social and political organizations. Segregation encouraged the development of a separate culture and ideology and is instrumental in reinforcing the salience of race and group status for individual African Americans (Dawson 1994). Table 2.1 shows the membership rates of legislators in major civil rights organizations by race and ethnicity. Civil rights organizations such as the National Association for the Advancement of Colored People (NAACP) and the National Urban League have a long history of engaging in political and legal action to increase opportunity for African Americans. As the table indicates, 27 percent of black members of Congress are members of civil rights organizations. Although these groups focus on the

TABLE 2.1
Membership Rate in Black Interest Major Civil Rights
Organizations by Race and Ethnicity, 107th Congress
(2001–2003)*

	% Membership in Black Interest Civil Rights Groups
Black[**] (n = 37)	27%
White (n = 375)	1.3%
Latino[**] (n = 19)	0%

*Major civil rights organizations include the traditional civil rights groups, the NAACP, National Urban League, Southern Christian Leadership Conference.
[**]Delegates are not included in this total.

TABLE 2.2
Membership Rate in Predominantly Black Fraternities
and Sororities, 107th Congress (2001–2003)

	% *Membership in Fraternities and Sororities*
Black* (n = 37)	25%
White (n = 375)	0%
Latino* (n = 19)	0%

*Delegates are not included in this total.

advancement of civil rights for minorities, their membership is not restricted to blacks. In fact, both whites and blacks were instrumental in the founding of the NAACP in the early 1900s.

Twenty-five percent of black legislators belong to predominantly black fraternities such as Omega Psi Phi, Alpha Phi Alpha, Kappa Alpha Psi, Phi Beta Sigma, and Iota Phi Theta and to predominantly black sororities such as Delta Sigma Theta, Alpha Kappa Alpha, Sigma Gamma Rho, and Zeta Phi Beta (table 2.2). These groups have policies and programs designed specifically to improve the social, political, and economic interests of blacks. Unlike many white college-based fraternities and sororities, members of black fraternities and sororities are encouraged to participate in community service activities throughout life that are designed to improve the conditions of blacks locally and nationwide. In fact, new members can become part of the organizations even after they graduate from college. In addition, a number of African American members of Congress attended historically black colleges, which also reinforce racial group identification, and a number of black legislators who attended predominantly white universities were members of majority-black student organizations aimed at promoting the collective interests of black students. In addition to fraternal groups, black legislators are often members of political black churches or churches to which political awareness and messages are central to the organizational mission (McClerking and McDaniel 2005). Political churches promote group identification as well as racial group consciousness among members (Calhoun-Brown 1996; McKenzie 2004).

In general, white legislators are not members of groups based solely on their racial background that stress the collective advancement of Caucasian Americans. Only 1.3 percent of white legislators belong to civil rights organizations (table 2.1). Nor is it likely that white legislators believe that their life chances are linked to those of other whites or to blacks. In addition, white legislators are not permitted to join many black organizations, such as the Congressional Black Caucus, which restrict membership to African Americans. The CBC has made a conscious decision to exclude whites from having full voting rights or membership in the caucus. Although white legislators who are supportive of the CBC's goals can maintain an associate membership or affiliation with the group, they are excluded from attending meetings or taking part in the agenda-setting process; this is reserved solely for black members of Congress. Although predominantly black fraternities and sororities are open to all racial groups, their memberships are almost all black. Not surprisingly, no white legislators are members of predominantly black fraternities or sororities (table 2.2).

While liberal white legislators may well support legislation that favors black Americans, then, their commitment to pro-black legislation is of a different sort than that of black legislators. Black members of Congress feel an obligation, based on a sense of common fate and reinforced in many cases by membership in black-identified political and social organizations, to represent a broader national constituency of blacks, other minorities, and the poor.

Origins of Strategic Group Uplift for Latino Legislators

Although much of the literature related to racial group consciousness has centered largely on blacks, existing research demonstrates that Latinos also possess an ethnic group consciousness (Garcia Bedolla 2009; Hero 1992; Sanchez 2006; Stokes 2003; Welch and Hibbing 1984). Ethnic group membership plays a significant role in determining the partisan and ideological attitudes of Latinos. Specifically, Latinos tend to be more liberal and more supportive of the Democratic Party than are whites (Welch and Sigelman 1993). Although Latinos are more diverse in terms of ideology and party affiliation than blacks, there is a strong reason to expect that ethnic group consciousness may play a role in predicting Latino policy preferences on many socioeconomic and ethnic issues. Scholars show that the policy preferences of Mexican Americans, Puerto Ricans, and Cubans do not vary significantly on various issues despite the heterogeneity that exists within and between these groups. Though Cuban Americans are more likely to express conservative views than Mexican Americans or Puerto Ricans, for example, they are still much in agreement about how to respond to perceived discrimination or threats to Latinos as a group (Leal 2007; Sanchez 2006). On issues such as support of bilingual education and immigration reform, these Latino subgroups have found commonality.

The ethnic group consciousness that exists among Latinos can be traced to their shared colonial past and to shared experiences of discrimination and segregation, which unites many Latinos beyond language. Chavez (2004) makes this point about Latinos of Mexican ancestry, but it is equally valid for other Spanish-speaking groups in the United States: "This complicated history of longtime resident status, history of persistent discrimination, and lasting disadvantaged socioeconomic and social stratification has created a relatively strong sense of cohesion and common identity among Mexican-origin Latinos" (25).

It seems likely that the ethnic group consciousness found in the Latino mass public extends to Latino legislators. Again, similar to black legislators, Latino legislators must balance their desire to be reelected against their commitment to advance the collective interests of Latinos nationally. Studies examining Latino legislators' activities on the state level find that Latino legislators are more likely than non-Latinos to sponsor Latino-interest bills (Bratton 2006). Like black members of Congress, Latino legislators identify with other Latinos, as reflected, for example, in the advocacy of Rep. José Serrano (D-NY) at a hearing before the Subcommittee on Early Childhood, Youth and Families of the Committee on Economic and Educational Opportunities pertaining to whether English should be the official language in the United States. Serrano, a Latino legislator from the Bronx, drew upon the Latino collective group experience in his objections to the English-language proposal:

> Now, I was born in Puerto Rico. I was born an American citizen. I speak Spanish. I speak English. I know what language I have to speak when I am before you, my colleagues. I know what language I have to write when I fill out my IRS income tax forms or when they call me up to find out my deduction for basketball shoes for last night's game. I have to know what language I speak. When Hispanics sit around the dinner table, we do not plot undoing the English language. We actually remind ourselves how our Pedro no longer speaks Spanish well and how Juanito, a grandchild, does not speak Spanish at all. (*Hearing on English as a Common Language*, 22)

As the example of Serrano also suggests, ethnic group consciousness extends beyond Latino subgroups. Even though Puerto Ricans have been US citizens since 1917 as a result of the Jones Act, Puerto Rican members of Congress such as Serrano, Luis Gutiérrez (D-IL), and Nydia Velazquez (D-NY) behave as though they feel a special obligation to help other Latinos who are not Puerto Ricans obtain citizenship.

Consistent with the survey research on political behavior, scholars have found that surrogate representation affects legislators' perceptions of and willingness to be active on policy issues. For example, Bill Richardson (D-NM), in his opening statement before the Subcommittee on Health and the Environment of the Committee on Energy and Commerce, professed to be "tremendously concerned about the health status of all minorities"— not just Latinos in his own district—in remarks before a hearing on primary care services for the underserved, and he focused his comments on the need to "move from a minority model of health care and recognize specific needs of Hispanic communities" in order to ensure that Hispanics received proper care (*Primary Care Services for the Underserved*, 2). In a similar vein, the Congressional Hispanic Caucus, founded in 1976, is organized to advocate for the interests of all Latinos in the United States and Puerto Rico, not just the interests of Latinos in individual districts. Representative Serrano, speaking as chairman of the CHC, made a similar point before the same committee, to whom he made comprehensive remarks regarding "demographic and socioeconomic characteristics that affect Hispanic health, the health status of Hispanic Americans, and barriers to full participation of Hispanic Americans in the health field" (12).

In addition to being in the CHC, Latino legislators are also more likely be members of major civil rights organizations that attend to Latino interests, such as the National Council of La Raza and the League of United Latin American Citizens (LULAC), than are white or black legislators. Table 2.3 shows that approximately 11 percent of Latino legislators belong to Latino-focused civil rights organizations, while no black or white legislators do. Similar to black fraternal organizations, Latino fraternal organizations such as Gamma Zeta Alpha, Lambda Alpha Upsilon, and Lambda Sigma Upsilon, and Latino sororities such as Alpha Phi Sigma

TABLE 2.3
Membership Rate in Latino Interest Major Civil Rights Organizations by Race and Ethnicity, 107th Congress (2001–2003)*

	% Membership in Latino Interest Civil Rights Groups
Latino** (n = 19)	11%
Black** (n = 37)	0%
White (n = 375)	0%

*Major civil rights organizations include the National Council of La Raza and the League of United Latin American Citizens.
**Delegates are not included in this total.

and Gamma Phi Omega, are dedicated to the collective uplift of Latinos. Since many of these groups were founded in the late 1980s, it is virtually impossible for Latino legislators in the 107th Congress (2001–2003) to have been members of these groups. An analysis of Latino legislators' biographies confirms that no Latino legislators were members of these organizations. Consequently, the groups played no role in influencing Latino legislators' ethnic group identity.

Hypotheses and Alternative Explanations

Given the likely salience of racial and ethnic group consciousness to black and Latino legislators, I make the following assumptions regarding strategic group uplift and individual legislator interventions in oversight activity, which I test in chapters 4 and 5:

> Hypothesis 1: As a result of strategic group uplift, black and Latino legislators are more likely than white legislators to intervene in explicitly racial hearings.
> Hypothesis 2: As a result of strategic group uplift, black and Latino legislators are more likely than white legislators to intervene in social welfare hearings.

Strategic group uplift may do much to explain why legislators intervene, but there are limits to how much it can explain. Some political philosophers have noted that one shortcoming of the notion that descriptive representatives provide better representation than nondescriptive representatives is the assumption that descriptive representatives advocate for interests of all members in the group (Phillips 1995; Young 2000). The concept of descriptive representation and other theories related to common or linked fate may mask the diversity that is present within a given group by suggesting that one representative can speak for everyone (Young 2000). Anne Phillips (1995) argues that class considerations are usually not accounted for in the politics of presence.

The empirical research among the public at large shows that although racial identity enables middle-class blacks to transcend their class positions on race issues, this political liberalism does not extend to the issues that do not involve race (Tate 1993). Even on race-related issues, political elites may pay more attention to advantaged individuals within the minority groups than to less advantaged ones (Cohen 1999; Strolovitch 2007). For example, although the CBC claims to represent the interests of all blacks, whether it will represent all minority interests is not clear. In *The Boundaries of Blackness* (1999), Cathy Cohen found that many members of the CBC failed to take an active role in advocating for legislative measures that specifically targeted the individuals most affected by HIV/AIDS in the African American community: gays, lesbians, and drug users. She found that many political leaders did not want to deal with these populations for fear that working with them would further marginalize the broader interests of the African American community. Another study found that although many leaders of civil rights groups like the NAACP expressed support for disadvantaged subgroups, they usually viewed political questions related to these groups, such as welfare policy, as being particularistic, while they viewed political questions related to advantaged subgroups, such as affirmative action, as being universal (Strolovitch 2007) .

This clarification suggests that black and Latino legislators may demonstrate distinctive preferences in oversight activities on issues that are salient to group interests—those that are explicitly racial in nature, such as civil rights and affirmative action laws—and less distinctive preferences on issues that are not as salient to the group, such as oversight of Medicaid or welfare spending. Thus, even though the racial identity of blacks enables them to transcend their middle-class positions to a certain extent, their political liberalism may extend only as far as addressing the problems of race, not to class inequalities (Tate 1993, 49). The strong unifying force of the CBC and CHC, however, should prompt black and Latino legislators to be unified in the positions they do take. The remaining sections in the chapter consider some competing explanations for this behavior.

Strategic Group Uplift and Ideology

Strategic group uplift is distinct from the Downsian liberal-conservative ideological spectrum that is used to capture mainly differences between Democrats and Republicans. Although legislators who are motivated to engage in congressional oversight of racial and social welfare policies tend to be liberal, as most black and Latino legislators are, possession of a liberal political ideology is not equivalent to possession of an orientation toward strategic group uplift.

Rep. John Conyers (D-MI) provides an illustration of the distinction. Most political observers are aware that Conyers is one of the most liberal members of Congress. No matter if the issue is civil rights or policies aimed at helping the poor, Conyers consistently receives the highest voting scores from liberal interest groups such as the Leadership Conference on Civil Rights. He has sponsored and continues to sponsor legislation that is controversial. He was the primary sponsor of the Martin Luther King holiday at a time when many Democrats were ambivalent about the bill, and for the past ten years Conyers has repeatedly introduced a bill requiring that the federal government pay African Americans reparations for slavery. He is also one of the founding members of the Congressional Black Caucus.

Conyers represents a district that is a liberal Democratic bastion. Blacks constitute more that 70 percent of the city's population and overwhelmingly throw their support to Democratic presidential candidates.

Given Conyers's reputation for liberalism, his advocacy for minority farmers may not come as a surprise. It is notable, however, that Conyers has been joined in this advocacy by considerably more conservative black and Latino legislators, including Sanford Bishop (D-GA) and Joe Baca (D-CA). Both Bishop and Baca are members of the Congressional Blue Dog Caucus; as Blue Dogs, they can be understood to be more fiscally and socially conservative than their fellow Democrats. To assess each member's mean ideological disposition, the first dimension of the Poole and Rosenthal DW-NOMINATE score is used. This score reflects each legislator's roll-call voting behavior on economic and social policies. The score is on a scale from 1 to –1, where a 1 is conservative and a –1 is liberal. In fact, Bishop, a black legislator representing Georgia, is the most conservative member in the CBC but is still a moderate member compared to other members in the full House, with an ideology score of –.206 as compared to Conyers's score of –.757. Baca, a Latino legislator representing California, falls at –.317. Unlike Conyers, Bishop and Baca serve on the House Agriculture Committee and have black and Latino farmers in their districts. Their advocacy for such farmers can be understood as a service to their own constituents or to black and Latino Americans more generally, but it cannot be understood solely as the product of their political ideology.

Constituency Influence

Many studies have found that the size of the black constituency in a district has a strong influence on how legislators vote on racial issues (Cameron, Epstein, and O'Halloran 1996; Hutchings, McClerking, and Charles 2004; Lublin 1997). As the number of blacks increases in a district, the voting record of its members of Congress becomes more liberal. Most studies use the size of the black voting-age population as a way to indicate constituent influence; however, this measure may not always adequately capture the degree of influence (see Fenno 1978; Kingdon 1989). The psychological attachments that black legislators have to their constituents add another dimension to understanding how legislators perceive constituents' interests. Although the number of potential black voters can have a significant effect on legislators' votes on highly salient issues, however, the effect is less significant for some legislators on less-salient votes (Hutchings, McClerking, and Charles 2004).

Although the number of potential voters in a district may have some impact on legislators' behavior, legislators' perceptions of who their constituents are may be more important than their numerical strength (Fenno

1978; Kingdon 1989; Miler 2010). Two legislators who have large black voting-age populations in their districts may not respond equally to their needs. Black and Latino legislators are more likely to notice their black and Latino constituents and to feel that their fates are linked to those of these group members. The issues that come before Congress directly affect the group; thus, these issues directly affect legislators.

Race/Ethnicity, Party Affiliation, and Leaders

The relationship between legislators' racial or ethnic background and party affiliation can be a vital factor influencing their likelihood of intervening in agency policymaking. Party affiliation is an important factor in determining legislators' support of various policies, affecting the way legislators vote, their level of participation in committee deliberations, and bills sponsored (Hall 1996; Kingdon 1989). Since the 1960s, Democrats have tended to be supportive of more liberal racial and social welfare policies than Republicans (Carmines and Stimson 1989; Lublin 1997). Due to racial and ethnic redistricting, as well as to the disappearance of conservative southern Democrats and their replacement by more liberal black southern Democrats, the Democratic Party has become more ideologically liberal in recent decades. The increase in the number of black and Latino representatives has contributed to the highest degree of ideological polarization ever recorded between the Democratic and Republican parties.

Nearly all of the time, black legislators are Democrats. They have more liberal voting records and ideologies than do Republican legislators. Although Democrats and Republicans differ in their level of support for various social and racial/ethnic policies, there are also intraparty differences among Democrats. After the 1960s, white liberals shifted their focus from the civil rights agenda to a more postmaterialist agenda (Berry 1999). Thus, racial policies divide Democrats, while they tend to agree more on social welfare and poverty issues. Thus, differences in policy preferences among black, Latino, and white Democrats should not be as pronounced on social welfare issues as they are on the explicitly racial issues. In fact, differences among the groups may be muted because black, white, and Latino legislators "carry the water" on these broader social welfare issues but not on the racial or ethnic issues.

The party affiliation of legislators and of the president is an important factor in determining legislators' likelihood of getting involved with agency oversight. Studies find that members' likelihood of intervening in bureaucratic policymaking decreases when their party holds the presidency, primarily because the president is more likely to espouse the same objectives as other members of his political party, leaving legislators free to spend their time and energy on other activities (Foreman 1988; Ogul 1976).

Conversely, the likelihood of oversight interventions by a legislator increases when the opposition party controls the presidency. Mayhew (1991) and other scholars find that the total number of oversight investigations does not change dramatically between divided and unified governments. Analysis of hearings concerned with racial and social welfare policy, however, shows that when Democrats are in control of the House, the number of hearings dedicated to racial/ethnic and social welfare issues is greater than when the Republicans are in control of the House. The Republican and Democratic parties usually have different perspectives on the ideal level of federal intervention in public policy matters. Republicans tend to espouse less government regulation and less intervention in social and economic affairs, whereas Democrats usually prefer more government intervention in these areas. When a Republican president is in power, Democratic legislators are more likely than Republicans to attend hearings and advocate for stronger enforcement of federal civil rights laws (Ogul 1976).

Party constraints limit the ability of black and Latino legislators to engage in the collective uplift of minority interests. While Democrats generally are more liberal than Republicans on the sort of racial and social welfare issues that benefit black and Latino constituents, these issues tend to divide the party. The party's agenda usually deemphasizes race and instead promotes race-neutral, class-based policies to remedy social inequities. The executive branch can reinforce this tendency: Democratic presidents Jimmy Carter and Bill Clinton, for example, distanced themselves from racial issues in their campaigns for the presidency. In the 1990s, President Clinton, in an effort to please conservatives within the Democratic Party, promised to make substantial changes to reform affirmative action and to radically reform welfare. The Congressional Black Caucus always introduces an alternative budget that calls for more resources to be directed toward eliminating inequities based on both race and class. Very few white Democrats ever vote for the CBC budget bill, while almost all black legislators do.

Cox and McCubbins (2005) have noted that parties can be central to the legislative process in Congress. All black legislators and all but two Latino legislators were Democrats in the 107th Congress (2001–2002). Black and Latino legislators can influence the agenda of the Democratic Party as well as the legislation that gets passed because they tend to vote in a cohesive bloc. Many white legislators work with minority members of Congress to help get issues addressed. The impact of the CBC and CHC therefore cannot be captured neatly by who is simply showing up at the hearings and participating; it must also consider the effect these actions have on white Democrats. For instance, coalitions may form with the result that party members, sometimes white members of Congress, attend hearings and articulate the viewpoint of a minority legislator because they have worked together with CBC or CHC members on the issues. This impact was noticed by Kingdon (1989) when he said many members are heavily influenced by other members of Congress on voting issues that they do not closely follow.

Electoral Safety of a District

It is common to argue that legislators who do not face real competition in election contests are less likely to be responsive to the needs and concerns of constituents than are those legislators who consistently compete against a credible challenger. In fact, many critics of partisan, racial, or ethnic redistricting have pointed to the 96 percent reelection rates of members of the US House of Representatives as evidence that elections are not effective tools for holding legislators accountable. "Safe" districts give legislators some degree of independence from their constituents, making them more likely to follow their own personal policy preferences to the detriment of their constituents. Following this logic, many skeptics of racial and ethnic redistricting argue that creating districts with substantial majorities of blacks and Latinos may increase the number of black and Latino representatives in Congress but do little to advance the substantive interests of black and Latino constituents in public policymaking (Swain 1993; Thernstrom 1987). Swain writes: "Another characteristic that marks many black representatives, especially those in historically and newly black districts (although it does not distinguish them from all members of the Congress), is they are relatively immune from an incentive that Mayhew and others view as central to congressional behavior—preoccupation with reelection. Black representatives from historically black districts are essentially guaranteed reelection if they survive their primaries. They have reelection rates exceeding even the high rate of House incumbents in general" (220). Indeed, the reelection rates and electoral margins show that black and Latino legislators are reelected at a higher rate than whites and with greater margins of victory.

Other studies have argued, on the flip side, that the fact that legislators from safe districts are consistently reelected indicates that they are very responsive to their constituents' concerns (Kingdon 1989). Legislators from the safe districts know that if they deviate too far from representing their constituents' interests, they may face a challenger in the next election (Arnold 1990). Even if incumbent legislators are not able to deter an opponent from running against them in an election, once they win, these legislators usually incorporate that challenger's main points of contention into their own legislative portfolio so they will not be challenged again on the same issue (Sulkin 2005). Nonetheless, legislators who win elections by large margins have some degree of independence from their constituents and are more likely to pursue their own policy interests than are legislators who win their contests by close margins.

Engaging in congressional oversight is not the best vehicle legislators can use to improve their odds of reelection and stave off potential election challengers, because most oversight activity takes place in the obscure halls of congressional hearings. Unlike roll-call votes, which draw the attention of interest groups that "score" legislators' voting in a variety of ways, few organizations, if any, keep track of how often legislators attend oversight hearings or how actively they engage in the deliberations in support of their decisions. Even when a legislator does actively engage in hearings, it would be difficult for his or her challenger to attribute any particular effect to this activity (Arnold 1990).

Black and Latino legislators from safe districts may have more latitude and flexibility to attend hearings and take positions on controversial issues, such as racial profiling and welfare reform, than do legislators from marginal districts. However, strategic group uplift motivates marginal minority legislators to behave in the same way as their safe counterparts. It ensures that legislators are responsive to the needs of their black and Latino constituents, because legislators believe that their constituents' fates are linked with their own. As a result, minority legislators from vulnerable districts are just as likely to engage in advocacy for black and Latino interests as are minority legislators from safe districts. To return to the example presented earlier in the chapter, Blue Dog Democrats such as black legislator Sanford Bishop and Latino legislator Joe Baca were just as likely to advocate for the interests of black and Latino farmers as were electorally safe legislators such as John Conyers.

Committee Leadership Positions

In general, committee leaders, whether they are chairs or ranking minority members, are more likely to participate in committee deliberations than are legislators at large (Hall 1996; Hall and Miler 2000; Ogul 1976). In addition to their individual office staff, these leaders have committee staff dedicated to gathering information and monitoring issues that concern the committee. Committee and subcommittee chairs have the power to set oversight agendas by scheduling hearings and calling witnesses to testify. Although they do not possess the same advantages as committee and subcommittee chairs, ranking minority members have a slightly larger staff and access to more resources in terms of committee information than do rank-and-file committee members. The extent to which black and Latino members hold powerful committee leadership positions therefore can play an important role in determining how much time they will spend intervening in agency policymaking. Black and Latino legislators who are on committees of interest in terms of racial or ethnic policy can spend more time setting up hearings that pertain to oversight of racial or social welfare issues than can white legislators. The ability to use a committee to set the agenda depends on whether Democrats control the House, however, because all blacks in the House of Representatives are Democrats.

Conclusion

Legislators' intervention in agency policymaking can be and often is vital to the substantive representation of constituent interests. By engaging in the deliberations of congressional committees responsible for overseeing federal agencies such as the Department of Justice or HUD, legislators are afforded an opportunity to communicate constituent concerns to federal officials in charge of implementing policies of critical importance to blacks and Latinos, such as racial profiling and welfare reform. Strategic group uplift plays a vital role not just in motivating legislators to intervene in agency policymaking but also in providing a voice to marginalized groups, such as blacks and Latinos, in congressional deliberations. Many political scientists and congressional scholars argue that legislators' activities tend to be structured around their self-interested desire to be reelected to office. Strategic group uplift provides a different way of examining legislators' motivations, focusing on how shared experiences interact with strategic factors to shape how they pursue their electoral goals.

Strategic group uplift motivates black and Latino legislators, more than non-minorities, to intervene in bureaucratic decision making because they have a vested interest in ensuring that agencies enforce policies that are favorable to the interests of their racial or ethnic group. Specifically, black and Latino legislators believe that their fate is linked with that of their black or Latino constituents, and they possess an ideology that holds that group members should engage in collective action to further the interests of the group. This ideology of racial or ethnic strategic group uplift greatly affects their perceptions of constituents and of what issues are important. Moreover, black and Latino legislators are likely to be members of identity caucuses, such as the CBC and CHC, which reinforce the philosophy that their members should engage in collective action to help blacks and Latinos. Thus, even when their constituents are not paying attention, black and Latino legislators are motivated to act in minority constituents' interest.

Although racial or ethnic group consciousness may motivate legislators' behavior related to explicitly racial or ethnic issues, existing research shows that it has limits in terms of addressing broader social welfare issues that disproportionately affect minorities. Black and Latino legislators will choose to be active on explicitly racial and ethnic issues that unify both middle-income and lower income blacks and Latinos, but they are likely to be less active on social welfare issues that tend to divide minority groups, such as welfare reform and poverty.

Before I assess the relationship between race or ethnicity of the legislator and its possible effect on involvement in oversight of agency policy by individual legislators, in chapter 3 I examine the history of congressional interventions in federal agency policymaking as it relates to the substantive representation of black and Latino interests. Specifically, I review congressional intervention in policy areas such as civil rights and social welfare. I pay particular attention to congressional efforts to ensure that federal agencies are enforcing or complying with these laws. The historical review provides the backdrop from which to analyze interventions by congressional committees in agency policy activities. While chapter 3 describes the uneven relationship between congressional intervention and enforcement of civil rights in federal policymaking as it relates to black substantive interests, it does not allow us to disaggregate the contributions by individual members of Congress in pursuing federal intervention in policies that are favorable to blacks and Latinos.

3

Congress, Minority Interests, and Federal Policymaking

THE FEDERAL GOVERNMENT'S commitment to protecting the rights of African Americans and Latinos has been uneven. At times it has played a strong role in protecting minorities against violations of their political, civil, and economic rights in the United States. For blacks, the end of the Civil War and the passage of several constitutional amendments by the Congress established citizenship and voting rights for former slaves. Blacks were formally incorporated into American civil society as equals; however, these freedoms would be short lived. As part of a compromise with Democrats, Republicans agreed to withdraw federal troops from the South in order to maintain their tenuous control of the presidency (Foner 1988). The troop withdrawal marked the official end of Reconstruction. During the ensuing period, Congress did very little to protect the civil rights of African Americans. Although individual legislators, mainly northern Republicans, introduced measures to stop political violence and intimidation and to eliminate restrictions on voting, such as the poll tax, Congress did not pass another civil rights bill until 1957.

Not only did the federal government abandon its commitment to civil rights, it did very little to improve the socioeconomic status of African Americans. The vast majority of former slaves were impoverished and had no means to maintain economic self-sufficiency. The Freedmen's Bureau was responsible for providing social welfare benefits and public schooling to blacks. Although many black Civil War veterans benefited from war pensions, most blacks did not receive social welfare benefits. During the Great Depression, blacks were largely excluded from New Deal relief programs, such as Social Security and unemployment insurance, mainly because of their race. Social programs designed to address socioeconomic disparities between blacks and whites were not implemented until the 1960s with the introduction of the Great Society.

The ability of the federal government to provide and protect civil rights for Latinos has been just as elusive as it has been for blacks. While Latino groups, including Mexican Americans, Puerto Ricans, and Cuban Americans, have all had distinct relationships with the federal government in their struggle for incorporation into civil society, the government's lack of commitment to providing civil rights and reducing socioeconomic inequalities has been similar across the subgroups. With the exception of Cubans, Latinos have been denied civil rights protections afforded to whites. Like blacks, Latinos were excluded from Depression-era relief programs. Moreover, Mexican Americans have been subject to deportations associated with immigration raids. Latinos, like blacks, did not receive a guarantee of their civil rights from Congress until the passage of civil rights legislation in the late 1950s.

Although the civil rights movement played a significant role in getting Congress to enact laws that removed barriers to voting, access to housing, and employment, subsequent efforts to enforce these laws posed a new challenge for civil rights advocates. Federal agencies such as the US Department of Justice (DOJ) and US Department of Housing and Urban Development (HUD) are responsible for implementing and enforcing the provisions that protect the voting rights of blacks, Latinos, and Asian Americans and ensure fair housing. In addition, federal agencies such as the US Department of Health and Human Services and HUD play a crucial role in administering many social welfare programs that assist the poor, who are disproportionately racial and ethnic minorities. Federal agencies have not always enforced civil rights laws or implemented social policies designed to improve the condition of blacks and Latinos. In fact, the US Equal Employment Opportunity Commission (EEOC) has long been criticized for its inability to effectively address and resolve employment discrimination complaints in a timely manner. Since many of the gains of the civil rights movement were codified into law, civil rights advocates and legislators have devoted considerable time to providing oversight of the federal bureaucracy. Although congressional committees are supposed to monitor federal agency compliance with civil rights and social welfare laws, history shows that Congress does not always do so and that it sometimes plays a significant role in hindering agencies from enforcing these laws (Walton 1988).

This chapter examines Congress's historical and contemporary role in overseeing the bureaucracy as it relates to enacting and implementing racial/ethnic and social welfare policies. Most of the congressional politics literature examines whether Congress as an institution pays attention to particular issues; rarely do studies examine to what extent individual legislators devote attention to these same issues by intervening in agency policymaking. This chapter offers a historical examination of the collective efforts of Congress and of individual legislators to advocate for the interests of racial and ethnic minorities during the eras of Reconstruction, the New Deal, and the Great Society by way of providing context for the analysis in the chapters that follow.

Congressional Intervention and African Americans

Congress can be a powerful force in providing protection for minority rights, whether by passing major legislation or using its vast oversight powers to ensure that federal agencies are implementing and enforcing current laws. Shortly after Reconstruction, Congress passed several federal election laws, or Force Acts, aimed at protecting the voting rights of blacks in the South as well as in the North. The US Department of Justice was the primary federal agency responsible for enforcing and implementing the Force Acts. Members in both chambers and both parties played a significant role in intervening in DOJ efforts to implement and enforce the laws. Most blacks, as well as congressional Republicans, supported the enforcement of civil rights laws aimed at reducing political violence and voter intimidation by Democrats and the Ku Klux Klan (Foner 1988). Thus, Republicans intervened in agency efforts in favor of stronger enforcement. Congressional Republicans led by Charles Sumner and Thaddeus Stevens used direct resources such as extra manpower and monies to increase the number of federal prosecutions of voting rights violations (James and Lawson 1999).

Blacks serving in Congress wanted the federal government to devote even greater effort to enforcing civil rights for the freedmen (Cobb and Jenkins 2001). Legislators in the Senate such as Hiram Revels (D-MS) and Blanche Bruce (D-MS) and legislators in the House such as Joseph Rainey (D-SC) and Robert Smalls (D-SC) advocated for social and economic policies that would improve the socioeconomic status of blacks. They introduced and supported legislation designed to provide greater access to public schooling and voting rights for blacks (Cobb and Jenkins 2001; Foner 1988). Black legislators had more liberal voting records than whites and strong preferences for these policies. They wanted the federal government to provide more economic relief and assistance to help improve the socioeconomic condition of blacks, while many white moderate Republicans believed that blacks did not deserve any special assistance from the federal government. In addition to pushing for more funding, black legislators engaged in congressional oversight activities on behalf of black interests. For example, Senator Bruce served as chairman of a Senate oversight committee responsible for investigating the failure of the Freedmen's Savings and Trust Company (Clay 1993). The committee found that banking officials were corrupt and were stealing money from the members, who were primarily ex-slaves (Clay 1993).

Southern Democrats, who were increasingly gaining power in the Congress, resisted the efforts of black and white liberal legislators to fight for black interests. In 1875 Democrats gained control of the US House of

Representatives for first time since the Civil War and used their newfound power to limit DOJ officials' enforcement of federal election laws. Specifically, congressional Democrats attached a series of riders to the Department of Justice's appropriations in an effort to reduce the amount of resources being expended on prosecutions under the Force Acts (Gillette 1979). The reduction in appropriations affected the number of employees that the agency could hire, decreasing its manpower and thereby limiting the number of cases that could be pursued by agency officials. Although the GOP wanted to protect the rights of freedmen, it wanted even more to hold on to the presidency. In the contested presidential election of 1876 between Republican candidate Rutherford B. Hayes and Democratic candidate Samuel J. Tilden, Republicans agreed to withdraw federal troops from the South; in return, Hayes would receive the electoral votes of the House Democrats, which would give him the election. The removal of the troops marked the official end of Reconstruction and, for several decades, of significant efforts to enforce minority civil rights protections.

In the subsequent years, Congress did little or nothing to protect black Americans from lynching, segregation, and other forms of political violence and intimidation (Carmines and Stimson 1989). Many state government enacted laws that disenfranchised blacks and limited other civil rights protections (Kousser 1974; Woodward 1955). Even the voices of ardent supporters of black civil rights were silenced: once Reconstruction ended, black members of Congress were forcefully removed from the body by white southerners. The battle for civil rights was waged in the courts instead of the Congress. In *Plessy vs Ferguson* (1896), the US Supreme Court approved the "separate but equal doctrine," which stated that the separation of races was permissible under law provided that both groups had equal access to similar resources. *Plessy* allowed for legal segregation of schools and public accommodations, such as hotels and restaurants. State governments also placed restrictions on voting, such as literacy tests, grandfather clauses, poll taxes, and white primaries. These restrictions made it difficult for African Americans to participate in the political process. Though civil rights groups such as the NAACP pursued strategies to keep racial issues on the national agenda, the prospects for greater federal protection of civil rights did not improve for many decades.

During the era of the Great Depression, a tenuous coalition between southern and northern Democrats provided the necessary support for New Deal programs. President Roosevelt did not want legislation addressing racial discrimination, because he feared that by backing such legislation he would lose the support of southern Democrats and thus jeopardize congressional support for his policies. Likewise, congressional Democrats could not advocate for blacks without losing southern support and endangering their advantage in Congress. Blacks switched their allegiance from the Republican Party to the Democratic Party partly because of the appeal of Franklin Roosevelt's New Deal policies, but members of Congress in the North were reluctant to intervene on behalf of blacks or racial policies from fear that their white constituents would oppose such policies (Carmines and Stimson 1989); thus "the congresses before Humphrey, Douglas, and Lehman produced no well-known advocates" of civil rights (62).

The presence of southern Democrats in key committee posts ensured that civil rights issues were not discussed in Congress. From 1930 through 1950, few, if any, congressional oversight hearings were conducted that examined the discriminatory practices of the Federal Housing Administration (FHA). Members of Congress were reluctant to introduce bills or take a position against the discriminatory practices at the FHA. It was not until 1959 that bills were introduced and hearings held on this issue.

The importance of maintaining the New Deal coalition may explain why many northern Democrats did not advocate openly for stronger action by Congress to intervene in the discriminatory policies of the New Deal era. Democratic President Franklin Roosevelt and congressional Democrats realized that in order to stay in power they had to appease both blacks, who were migrating to the North and voting Democratic, and white southerners who opposed civil rights and the inclusion of blacks in the governmental programs. Cognizant of this tenuous coalition, Roosevelt and most Democrats avoided taking a position or advocating for civil rights legislation. For example, the NAACP advocated for legislation to make lynching and other forms of political violence against blacks a federal crime. Although antilynching legislation was introduced in Congress through more than 150 bills from 1870 to 1900, none of the bills became law (Carmines and Stimson 1989).

The NAACP and other civil rights organizations also wanted Congress to introduce legislation that eliminated barriers to voting for blacks. Although Congress held legislative hearings addressing the use of such devices as literacy tests and poll taxes, the hearings did not succeed in producing positive change. Southern legislators controlled the agenda of the committees responsible for intervening in agency policymaking and effectively limited the debate on civil rights and oversight of agencies responsible for enforcing these laws. Zelizer (2004) explains the extent of Southern dominance on committees: "Southerners also chaired almost 50 percent of the House and Senate committees, since they constituted almost 50 percent of the Democratic Party throughout this era. Southern Democrats claimed 48 percent of Senate chairs and ranking minority posts from 1933 to 1952, and 51 percent in the House" (22).

Additionally, it was very difficult for blacks to work through the system to get their concerns heard, because the majority of blacks resided in the districts and states that were controlled by southern Democrats who were opposed to the extension of civil rights to black people. Most advocacy for minority interests came from organized groups such as the NAACP and the National Black Women Organization (Hamilton and Hamilton 1997). In their fight for civil and social welfare justice, civil rights groups had strong working relationships with very few senators. Only two black legislators served in Congress during this time period, both in the House: Oscar DePriest (R-IL, 1929–1935) and Arthur Mitchell (D-IL, 1935–1943). Representative Mitchell of Illinois, the first black Democrat to serve in Congress, delivered a House floor speech criticizing state administration of public assistance and calling for greater federal financing and control (Lieberman 1998).

Civil Rights for Blacks in the Postwar Era

Many African Americans served in World Wars I and II, and they demanded the benefits that white veterans received as a result of their service. In addition, blacks who had migrated to the North in great numbers supported Democratic candidates. The push for reform in Congress, along with the civil rights movement demanding redress from the federal government, forced legislators to pay attention to civil rights issues. For much of this period, intervention on behalf of minorities was conducted mainly by presidents and the courts, with Congress not doing much to advance the issues; however, this began to change in the late 1940s. In 1948, President Truman desegregated the military; he subsequently supported the first comprehensive civil rights bill introduced in Congress since Reconstruction. The bill's provisions included making racial lynching a federal crime, strengthening voting rights for blacks, and providing antidiscrimination laws in housing and employment. The bill also called for the creation of the Fair Employment Practices Commission. The proposal stalled in the Senate because of the opposition of southern Democrats such as Senator Strom Thurmond (D-SC). Many conservative Democrats were angry that the Democratic Party had taken action on civil rights. Thurmond left the Democratic Party and ran for president as a candidate for the States' Rights Party. Truman won the election but lost every former confederate state in the presidential contest.

The large migration of blacks to northern urban areas had gradually increased their importance to the northern Democratic coalition and led to a greater focus on civil right issues by Democrats. Well-known advocates for civil rights joined Congress during the late 1940s and the 1950s. Northern liberals such as John Kennedy introduced civil rights legislation, and Hubert Humphrey and Everett Dirksen became strong voices for minority rights, introducing legislation and intervening on behalf of civil rights groups to get federal agencies to treat minorities fairly. The first goal of many northern liberals was to change the committee system, which stymied both civil rights advocacy and the passage of labor union legislation (Zelizer 2004). The push for reform of institutions in Congress, along with the momentum of the civil rights movement, forced Congress to respond to the concerns of minorities. This response began with the creation of the Civil Rights Division of the Department of Justice in 1957. Subsequently, Congress passed the Civil Rights Act of 1964 and the Voting Rights Act of 1965.

The Civil Rights Act has been amended several times since its original passage. In addition to removing many of the political barriers that disenfranchised blacks for almost a century, the legislation created new federal agencies, including the Department of Housing and Urban Development (HUD) and the Equal Employment Opportunity Commission (EEOC), to combat discrimination in housing and employment, respectively. In 1968, Congress passed the Fair Housing Act to protect minorities against discrimination in housing, which gave HUD the responsibility for mediating housing disputes and made the Department of Justice responsible for litigating any housing complaints. The act also charged existing federal agencies with enforcing various civil rights provisions that protected the civil and voting rights of blacks.

Again, southern legislators who had powerful leadership positions on key congressional committees fought against the passage of the legislation and sought to limit the ability of federal agencies to implement its provisions by, for example, passing budgets that deliberately omitted the funds necessary to oversee civil rights responsibilities effectively (Ogul 1976). The Nixon administration refused to ensure that federal agencies adequately implemented civil rights provisions. In the 90th Congress (1967–1969), there were only five black legislators serving in the House; however, during the 91st Congress (1971–1973), the number had increased to thirteen (Amer 2004). The infusion of black legislators into the House put pressure on Congress to focus on maintaining the gains of the civil rights movement.

After progress in terms of inclusion and getting the federal government to be responsive to civil rights, the resulting federal legislation had to be implemented by the federal bureaucracies. Some have found that, in addition to Congress's ability to affect federal agencies' efforts to implement civil rights legislation, these bureaucracies have not been proactive in enforcing civil rights provisions. For example, in *When the Marching Stopped*, Walton (1988) found that federal agencies did not enact the necessary rules to implement Title VI of the Civil Rights Act, which prohibits discrimination by entities that receive federal funds. Agencies such as the EEOC and HUD, which were created to enforce equal employment opportunity laws and fair housing laws, respectively, encountered difficulty enforcing the laws due to lack of funding and political will.

Discrimination in Federal Economic Relief Programs

The mid-twentieth century also witnessed a shift in congressional treatment of black social welfare. During the Great Depression, federal agencies such as the Social Security Administration, the Federal Housing Administration (FHA), and the Veterans Administration (VA) were created by Congress to provide relief to citizens, but these agencies excluded African Americans from receiving benefits. FHA and VA loans made home ownership more accessible to citizens by reducing the down payment necessary for purchasing a home: by providing loan guarantees to mortgage lenders, the federal government enabled qualified home borrowers to invest only a 5 percent down payment for a home instead of the 20 percent required for a conventional bank loan. Although the federal subsidies were supposed to benefit all people who were eligible, blacks were systematically excluded from participating in these programs by private lenders and by the federal agencies themselves. Banks refused to provide loans on properties in racially mixed and all-black neighborhoods, and the FHA and VA assigned these communities low ratings that made the properties in them ineligible for federally insured loans. FHA guidelines stated that communities had to be either all white or all black in order for their residents to receive assistance; the FHA's *Underwriting Manual* directed that racially segregated communities were necessary in order to maintain neighborhood stability. By refusing to provide loans to people in inner cities, the FHA encouraged middle-class whites to move to the suburbs and significantly contributed to inner-city decline (Massey and Denton 1993). Consequently, it is widely held that FHA policies of the 1930s-1950s greatly contributed to the residential segregation patterns that exist in 2000s (Massey and Denton 1993). Researchers estimate that blacks lost billions of dollars due to this policy (Oliver and Shapiro 1995).

Congress also did little to combat widespread discrimination against blacks in employment. Blacks were systematically excluded from defense industry jobs that were created as a result of the buildup to World War I. Civil rights leaders such as A. Philip Randolph threatened mass protests if the defense industry did not hire and employ more blacks (Hamilton and Hamilton 1997). Some scholars attribute Randolph's threat to march on Washington as the primary reason for President Franklin Roosevelt's decision to issue an executive order to fight discrimination in employment and to establish the Fair Employment Commission.

In the 1930s blacks were effectively excluded from participating in the Old Age Insurance and Unemployment Insurance programs created by the Social Security Act because employers of agricultural workers and domestic servants were not required to cover their workers. Since blacks and Latinos fell disproportionately in the agriculture and domestic service categories, they were not eligible to receive assistance. Although the NAACP lobbied for the inclusion of agricultural and domestic workers and for making blacks eligible for unemployment insurance, southern Democrats in Congress opposed their inclusion. Some legislators in Congress introduced amendments to include agricultural workers and domestic servants, but these amendments failed to garner widespread support. Blacks in need of support from the government thereby fell under the second-tier, need-based assistance program known as Aid to Dependent Children (ADC). The administration of ADC was delegated mainly to the states, even though civil rights groups wanted the federal government to administer the program for fear that state governments would exclude blacks. As civil rights organizations feared, southern state governments proceeded to discriminate against and even exclude blacks as program recipients. Finally, in 1950, Congress amended the Social Security Act to make agricultural workers and domestic servants eligible for old-age and survivors insurance (Hamilton and Hamilton 1997; Lieberman 1998). This move made it possible for black Americans to received aid that was federally administered and did not carry the same stigma as need-based assistance.

In the 1960s a number of liberal social welfare programs were passed by Congress and signed into law. These broad, sweeping social welfare programs were designed to address poverty by extending need-based aid to more families and providing health insurance to the elderly and the poor through the programs Medicare and Medicaid. Liberal senators such as Edward Kennedy (D-MA), Joseph Clark (D-PA), and Jacob Javits (R-NY) were supportive of civil rights and social welfare legislation. They advocated for stronger enforcement of civil rights legislation and more funding for antipoverty programs (Hamilton and Hamilton 1997).

Although these Great Society programs represented a significant accomplishment for civil rights groups, the election of Richard Nixon, an opponent of civil rights and of spending on social welfare programs, demonstrated the strong resistance of many in the nation to liberal social welfare policies. The Nixon administration, with the support of southern Democrats, tried to dismantle or scale back Great Society initiatives such as school lunches, nutrition programs for children, job training, and college loans and grants (Clay 1993).

The resistance to the implementation of civil rights and social welfare policies gave rise to many liberal congressional caucuses aimed at protecting the gains of the civil rights movement. Perhaps the most visible, the Congressional Black Caucus (CBC), was founded in 1971 to help promote the interests of all blacks in the nation. The increase in the number of black members in Congress, especially in the House of Representatives, made it possible for legislators to pool their resources and advocate for minority interests in Congress. Before the CBC, black Americans relied primarily on civil rights organizations such as the NAACP and liberal white legislators to advocate for their interests in government. With the formation of the CBC, blacks gained advocates who not only introduced and voted on important legislation but also played an active role in overseeing the enforcement of civil rights and the implementation of social welfare policies. Part of the CBC's charge was to ensure that the Nixon administration would not eliminate programs that served the interests of blacks. These legislators played an instrumental role in calling for hearings to monitor the status of civil rights enforcement. As Walton (1988) found, Congressman Augustus Hawkins called for hearings to ensure that agencies were indeed implementing civil rights laws. As chair of the House Committee on Education and Labor's Subcommittee on Employment Opportunities, Hawkins demanded stronger enforcement of equal employment opportunities laws, and he argued that agencies should reduce or eliminate the funding from organizations that violated provisions of the Civil Rights Act. Legislators such as John Conyers (D-MI) and Charles Rangel (D-NY) testified at hearings demanding full employment and requesting that unemployment in inner-city neighborhoods be addressed. Black members of Congress continued to provide advocacy for the poor and minorities when critics of welfare wanted to eliminate their benefits. At present, black and Latino legislators serve in Congress in sufficient numbers to advocate effectively for minority interests, and they do.

The historical view demonstrates the importance of congressional intervention in federal policymaking and of proper oversight of the agencies responsible for enforcing these laws. The extent to which Congress effectively oversees agency policymaking and makes agencies accountable has real consequences, especially in terms of providing a voice to groups that would not otherwise be heard. Whether at present these agencies are properly implementing current legislation and whether representatives are engaged in effective oversight is subject to much debate. Public opinion polls show that racial discrimination and civil rights issues still rank high among African Americans in terms of policy significance (Smith and Seltzer 2000).

While the history of the federal bureaucracy has been well documented for African Americans, less has been written regarding Latinos. There is some overlap between blacks and Latinos in terms of discrimination in housing and employment. However, Latinos have a history with the federal government that differs from that of blacks, and this history varies by Latino subgroup. The next section will examine this history.

Mexican Americans and the Federal Government

The United States gained most of Mexico's northern territory, what is now the American Southwest, as a result of their victory in the United States. Mexican War. In the 1848 Treaty of Guadalupe Hidalgo, the US government promised to grant US citizenship and civil and political rights to Mexicans in the conquered territories. As a result, Mexican Americans are the largest Latino subgroup in the United States, followed by Puerto Ricans and Cubans. Although Mexican nationals became US citizens, many of the white settlers who moved into the territories discriminated against Mexican Americans and denied them civil and political rights. Mexican Americans were not allowed to vote and had high rates of poverty. They were also victims of restrictive covenants contained in real estate transactions (Garcia Bedolla 2009). Anglo-Americans passed laws that prohibited Mexicans from frequenting restaurants and local shops (Chavez 2004).

The US demand for cheap labor has played a significant role in shaping the federal government's relationship with Mexican Americans. As a result, federal immigration policy has been and continues to be a key interest of Mexican Americans. During times of national crises and economic hardship, the US federal government detained and deported illegal Mexican aliens and sometimes also Mexican American citizens. During the Depression, President Herbert Hoover ordered stricter enforcement of immigration laws. Hoover believed that Mexicans were taking jobs from "real" Americans (Hoffman 1974). The US Labor Department's Bureau of Immigration searched for Mexicans or anyone who looked Mexican in order to detain or deport them. The tactics of the bureau were roundly criticized by newspapers and by local groups. Between 1929 and 1937, approximately 458,039 Mexicans were repatriated to Mexico; approximately 60 percent of the children who were repatriated were US citizens (Hoffman 1974). An analysis of the congressional hearings from these years shows that members of Congress did very little to defend Mexican Americans from the bureau's tactics, which many regarded as illegal. In fact, much of the rhetoric used in the congressional deliberations was hostile to Mexican immigration. During this period, only six Latinos served in Congress, four in the House and two in the Senate.[1]

This would not be the last time the federal government sanctioned the detaining and deportation of Mexican nationals and Mexican Americans.

---

[1] Both legislators in the Senate came from New Mexico: Octaviano Larrazolo (R-NM), the first Latino elected to the Senate, and Dennis Chavez (D-NM). All but one of the House members were the resident commissioners from Puerto Rico: José Lorenzo Pesquera, Santiago Iglesias, and Bolívar Pagán. The exception was Joachim Fernández (D-LA).

In the 1950s economic recession following the Korean War, the Immigration and Naturalization Service (INS) conducted "Operation Wetback," which removed approximately 1.3 million Mexicans from the United States (Chavez 2004; Hoffman 1974). As in the 1930s, few members of Congress spoke up against Operation Wetback or against the possibility that Mexican-American citizens were being detained. INS allowed illegal Mexican residents to cross the border, then arrested them and delivered them to work for various growers in Texas and the rest of the United States (Navarro and Meija 2004).

Puerto Ricans and the Federal Government

The colonial past has defined the relationship between the United States and Puerto Rico. Puerto Rico is a territory of the United States, and Puerto Ricans are US citizens through the Jones Act (1917), though they cannot vote in US federal elections. Their representative in Congress is a nonvoting resident commissioner. Previously, the resident commissioner could vote in the Committee as a Whole, but in 1995 the Republican-controlled Congress stripped the commissioner of this standing. Although many Puerto Ricans migrated to the United States in the early 1900s to work in agriculture industries, such as cotton and grape production in the western states, the largest migration of Puerto Ricans to the US mainland occurred because of labor shortages created by World War I. Puerto Ricans' social conditions and political interests have been more closely aligned with those of blacks than with those of any other Latino group. In terms of socioeconomic status, they suffer from poverty, substandard housing, high unemployment rates, and discrimination in employment at rates similar to (and sometimes higher than) blacks. As US citizens, however, Puerto Ricans have not been subject to deportation as many Mexicans and Mexican Americans have been.

Heavily concentrated in agriculture, Puerto Ricans were also excluded from unemployment and retirement insurance. Puerto Ricans tend to live in segregated communities and are victims of discrimination (Grosfoguel 2003). In the 110th Congress, there were four members of Puerto Rican descent: Delegate Carlos Romero-Barcelo, Rep. Nydia Velazquez (D-NY), Rep. Luis Gutiérrez (D-IL), and Rep. Jose Serrano (D-NY). Puerto Ricans are strong supporters of bilingual education and of ensuring that cities provide instruction to recent immigrants to ease their transition into civil society. They have also been strong supporters of civil rights voting protections, including the printing of ballots in more than one language. They have tended to vote overwhelmingly for Democrats and to support liberal social welfare programs.

Cuban Americans and Federal Government Intervention

The federal government's efforts to incorporate Cubans into American civil society have been complex. The federal government devoted extensive time and resources to incorporating the first wave of Cuban exiles into mainstream society—arguably more so than any other Latino group, and more so than for later waves of Cuban exiles. The first wave of Cubans emigrated to the United States in the 1950s and 1960s as a result of the Cuban Revolution and their forced exile by Fidel Castro. These early Cuban emigrants were mainly upper- and middle-income individuals who had ties to the deposed Batista regime (Chavez 2004). Cubans were racially categorized as "whites," and they received substantial assistance from the US federal government, in part because the federal government had a Cold War interest in ensuring that political exiles from Cuba prospered in the United States. Civil rights issues, such as discrimination in employment, housing, and lending, were not as salient with Cubans as they were with Mexican Americans and Puerto Ricans. The US government provided many services to help Cuban exiles adjust to US society. Cubans received favorable treatment obtaining citizenship that was not afforded to Mexican immigrants. Cuban businesses were able to thrive because they were provided SBA loans at higher rates than the businesses of Mexican immigrants and Puerto Ricans. Grosfoguel (2003) notes that "between 1968 and 1979, Cubans received approximately 46.9 percent ($47.6 million) of the total dollar amount of loans by the Small Business Administration (SBA) in Miami, compared to just 6.3 percent ($6.4 million) for African Americans during the same period" (85). Although Cubans are economically more prosperous than blacks and other Latino groups, they still lag behind Anglos in many socioeconomic indicators (Grosfoguel 2003).

Subsequent waves of Cuban emigrants have not received similar treatment from the US government. The later waves that came as a result of the Mariel boatlift consisted of lower- to middle-income individuals (Chavez 2004; Garcia Bedolla 2009). These exiles were poorer than previous waves of Cuban immigrants and reportedly included a higher proportion of the mentally ill and criminals. Responding to unpopular public opinion against this new wave of immigrants, President Jimmy Carter removed the refugee status from these exiles that had been afforded to previous Cuban exiles. The removal of refugee status meant these exiles were provided very little government assistance compared to the first wave of emigrants (Garcia Bedolla 2009).

Though Cuban emigrants tend to take a conservative stance on foreign policy against Castro, they are strong supporters of bilingual education and support fair immigration laws (Leal 2007). As the exile generation starts to get older, the younger generation is becoming more liberal on social welfare policies and forming coalitions based on racial identity. The Cuban delegation in Congress is still predominantly Republican, but the policy preferences of Cubans are gradually coming to be in line with those of other Latinos. Most Cuban Americans' preferences for bilingual education, elimination of linguistic barriers to electoral voting, and immigration are consistent with those of other Latino subgroups (Leal 2007). These preferences differ dramatically from those of Anglos. Cuban legislators have actively intervened on behalf of their constituents in terms of advocacy for language interests.

Federal Interventions and Latino Interests

Although Mexican Americans, Puerto Ricans, and Cubans are diverse in terms of their national origin and party affiliation, their shared history of unequal, discriminatory treatment has been instrumental in creating a Latino identity and interests. Many states denied Latinos civil rights protections and access to social welfare programs that were afforded to most non-Hispanic whites. The federal government did little to ensure the Latinos could fully participate in the political system and benefit from relief programs. Mexican Americans in the Southwest and Puerto Ricans in the Northeast were not granted the right to vote and encountered ethnic discrimination in housing and employment (Garcia Bedolla 2009). Latinos, like blacks, were excluded from many Depression-era relief programs, such as Social Security and unemployment insurance. Although Latinos also experienced barriers to voting similar to those that blacks encountered, such as poll taxes and literacy tests, linguistic barriers took on a more significant role in preventing Latinos from fully participating in the electoral system. Many first-generation Latinos are Spanish speakers, and election officials only provided campaign and election material in English, thus making it difficult for them to participate in the electoral process. Even Cuban Americans, who did not experience the same level of ethnic discrimination as Mexican Americans and Puerto Ricans, were affected by the lack of election materials in Spanish. Latinos were also denied equal access to quality public schools that would help immigrant children learn English.

Scholars have found that most Latino subgroups share similar views on the role of government, as well as on health care and language policy. Immigration is the main issue on which there is some divergence: whereas more than 80 percent of Mexican, Cuban, and Central and South Americans believe that immigration should be increased or kept the same, only 64 percent of Puerto Ricans responded the same way (Leal 2007). Latinos have policy views distinctive from those of Anglos on language and education, immigration, and civil rights policy (Leal 2007). The following sections focus on the issues on which issues the groups share common views.

Bilingual Education and Voting Rights Policy

Federal policy relating to voting rights and bilingual education has played an instrumental role in unifying the different Latino subgroups in their pursuit of political power and in providing access to education. Political scientist Ronald Schmidt Sr., in *Pursuing Power: Latinos and the Political System,* provides a detailed chronology of government efforts to provide bilingual programs for Latinos. In 1968 Congress passed the Bilingual Education Act as an amendment to the Elementary and Secondary Education Act (Title VII). The law's primary sponsor, Senator Ralph Yarborough (D-TX), was particularly interested in providing federal support for local bilingual education programs in south Texas that were aimed at stemming the relatively high drop-out rates and low educational attainment rate of Latino students). In 1974 the US Supreme Court ruled that teaching students in a language they did not understand violated the Civil Rights Act of 1964. As a result of the court's decision, in 1975 the US Office of Education's civil rights unit issued guidelines requiring school districts with sufficient numbers of non-English speakers to establish bilingual programs). In the 1980s, William Bennett, secretary of education in the Reagan administration, wanted to dismantle many of the bilingual programs for children with "limited English proficiency" (Schmidt 1997). Many congressional Democrats supported continued federal funding for bilingual education , and in 1988 75 percent of Title VII funds were reserved for transitional bilingual education. Schmidt explains what happened next: "Subsequently, both Presidents George Bush and Bill Clinton appointed educational administrators who were committed to retaining a federal commitment to bilingual education. . . . At state and local levels, meanwhile, vocal and unresolved political conflicts over bilingual education continued into the mid-1990s, with Latinos continuing to play a major part in the controversies" (346).

Several Latino political groups, led by the Mexican American Legal Defense and Education Fund, also lobbied Congress to amend the Voting Rights Act (1965) to include protections for language minorities (Schmidt 1997). In 1975 the Voting Rights Act was amended to include language provisions that made it possible for Spanish-speaking individuals to receive campaign and election material in either Spanish or English if more than 5 percent of the voters in the district spoke the same non-English language and if the English illiteracy rate in the district was greater than the national illiteracy rate (Schmidt 1997). Latino members of Congress, such as Rep.

Edward Roybal (D-CA), testified and advocated for the inclusion of Latinos under the Voting Rights Act.

Much of the discrimination encountered by blacks during the 1950s and 1960s was experienced also by Latinos in the areas of housing, employment, and lending. Latino activists sought greater federal protection in the provision of public social services, in the courtroom, and from employment discrimination, all by extending the protection granted to language minorities.

Latino legislators have testified and advocated for the inclusion of Latinos in employment as a way of raising their standard of living. The National Council of La Raza and LULAC, similar to other liberal groups, believe that guaranteeing a living wage would eliminate the poverty that exists in these communities. The Congressional Hispanic Caucus was formally organized to protect the interests of Hispanics in the United States in 1976. That year, only five Latino members served in Congress compared to the twenty-five that serve in 2009. Representatives of the CHC have testified at hearings and advocated for Congress to focus more attention on minority issues.

Federal Attention to Racial and Social Welfare Policies

Whether in passing the Voting Rights Act to guarantee the right to vote for blacks or in amending the act to ensure that language minorities such as Latinos are granted the same rights, the federal government has played an important role in determining whether civil rights and social welfare policies will respond to the needs of African Americans and Latinos. Federal civil rights legislation specifies an important enforcement and implementation role for federal agencies as well as state entities. Table 3.1 shows the employment discrimination cases filed with the EEOC based on race, sex, age, and disability. The long-standing demand of civil rights advocates and minority constituents is that the agency be more vigorous in the enforcement of the law by resolving more complaints more rapidly through the administrative vehicles at the EEOC. Discrimination complaints based on race represent the greatest percentage of cases handled by the EEOC, followed next by sex and age discrimination.

The federal bureaucracy also plays an important role in the implementation of social welfare policies. Most minorities have received benefits only from second-tier, need-based social welfare programs such as Temporary Aid for Needy Families (TANF), not from social insurance programs such as Social Security. Tables 3.2 and 3.3 show the percentage of persons receiving Medicaid and TANF benefits by racial and ethnic background. The federal government plays an important role in determining the deposition

TABLE 3.1

Equal Employment Opportunity Commission Discrimination Complaints by Selected Category, FY 2008

	% of Total Charges
Race	35.6%
Sex	29.7%
Age	25.8%
Disability	20.4%
N = 95,402*	

Source: U.S. Equal Employment Opportunity Commission: http://www.acf.hhs.gov/programs/ofa/character/FY2006/tab08.htm

*The number for total charges reflects the number of individual charge filings. Because individuals often file charges claiming multiple types of discrimination, the number of total charges for any given fiscal year will be less than the total of the eight types of discrimination listed.

of the programs and defining how states are to implement them. Blacks and Latinos disproportionately receive these program benefits, with blacks representing 12 percent of the US population and Hispanics representing 14 percent. These agencies have enacted several rules that have disproportionately affected African Americans, by, for example, reducing who is eli-

TABLE 3.2

Percent Distribution of Temporary Assistance for Needy Families by Race/Ethnicity, October 2005–September 2006

	% of TANF Recipients
Black	35.7%
White	21.8%
Hispanic	26.1%
Other	7.2%
N = 1,802,567	

Source: U.S. Equal Employment Opportunity Commission: http://www.acf.hhs.gov/programs/ofa/character/FY2006/tab08.htm

TABLE 3.3
United States: Distribution of the Nonelderly with
Medicaid by Race/Ethnicity 2007

	% of Medicaid Recipients
White	44%
Black	21.8%
Hispanic	27%
Other	7.2%
N = 36,359,410	

Source: Kaiser Family Foundation: http://www.statehealth
facts.org

gible for Medicaid services and TANF services. In 1996 welfare reform
enacted work requirements and made it difficult for blacks and Latinos to
get benefits.

Conclusion

History shows that, over time, congressional advocacy for the civil rights
and social welfare of blacks and Latinos has varied often. In the Reconstruction era, white legislators such as Charles Sumner and Thaddeus Stevens and black legislators such as Hiram Revels, Blanche Bruce, Joseph
Rainey, and Robert Smalls advocated for the civil rights of African Americans. The end of Reconstruction in the South coincided with diminished
advocacy for minority rights in Congress; for many decades, only a few
interest groups spoke up for minority rights in Congress. It was not until
the rise of congressional liberals such as Hubert Humphrey in the 1940s
and 1950s that forceful advocates for civil rights for minorities returned to
Congress. The historical record speaks to the value of the interventions of
such individual legislators. By engaging in deliberations and requesting
hearings on behalf of minorities, liberal legislators play a valuable role in
representative democracy. These congressional advocates played a key role
in the deliberative process to keep the issues alive and well. Whether by
attending oversight hearings, introducing bills, or participating in deliberations on the House or Senate floor, these legislators provided an important voice to minority citizens. Although they were not able to get antilynching legislation passed or to immediately eliminate discrimination in
employment or in the voting booth, these individual legislators were vital

allies to interest groups that were fighting for civil rights. The federal government has and continues to play an important role in protecting the civil rights of blacks and Latinos and ensuring that minorities are included in social welfare programs. However, from 1879 through the late 1960s, there were few black and Latino legislators in Congress. In fact, at the passage of the Civil Rights Act (1964), only five blacks and four Latinos served in the House of Representatives. With few descriptive representatives in Congress, blacks and Latinos had to rely primarily on minority advocacy groups such as the NAACP and on liberal white legislators sympathetic to minority interests to advocate for them.

Demographic changes and racial redistricting have resulted in a dramatic increase in the number of minorities serving in Congress. In the 110th Congress (2007–2009), there were forty-two black legislators and twenty-three Latino legislators. The proponents of racial redistricting have argued that the increased presence of minority legislators in Congress should lead to a federal government that is more responsive to minority needs. Since more minority representatives have a critical mass in the Congress, it is logical to assume that black and Latino legislators should be more proactive and vigorous in their advocacy of civil rights enforcement than white legislators. In analyzing whether or not this is the case, most of the historical account regarding minority advocacy is anecdotal. The following chapters systematically address whether the inclusion of more black and Latino legislators in Congress has led to greater responsiveness by individual legislators to minority interests in the enforcement of civil rights and the implementation of social welfare policies.

4

Black and Brown Voices in Committee Deliberations on Civil Rights

DURING MUCH of the 1980s, black and Latino legislators, with the support of civil rights organizations such as the NAACP and the National Council of La Raza, complained that President Ronald Reagan and President George H. W. Bush had abandoned the federal government's commitment to enforcing civil rights laws. They accused the Reagan and Bush administrations of appointing directors who were not sympathetic to charges of racial or ethnic discrimination, the most prominent being future US Supreme Court justice Clarence Thomas. Civil rights advocates argued that agencies such as the Equal Employment Opportunity Commission (EEOC) failed to resolve many of the racial and ethnic discrimination complaints filed by employees against their employers. In addition, the EEOC referred fewer discrimination complaints to the US Department of Justice (DOJ) than the Carter administration had. When in 1992 Bill Clinton defeated George H. W. Bush in the US presidential contest, he promised to "mend and not end" policies such as affirmative action. For many civil rights organizations, the election of the first Democratic president since Jimmy Carter presented a new opportunity to renew the executive branch's commitment to the vigorous enforcement of civil rights laws.

In addition to a new president, black and Latino legislators were elected at historic rates to the US Congress in 1992. Civil rights groups believed that the president and Congress would encourage the nation to direct more attention to racial issues. These groups wanted the DOJ to file more class-action lawsuits against employers in the private and public sector. The Clinton administration satisfied this key constituency by vigorously enforcing antidiscrimination laws. The DOJ's Civil Rights Division filed and won major racial discrimination lawsuits against Denny's restaurants and Texaco Oil. The EEOC processed and resolved discrimination complaints at a higher rate than it had under the previous Republican administrations.

With the increase in the number of black and Latino legislators in the House, congressional committees also held hearings that addressed allegations of discrimination and unfair treatment by federal agencies. Legislators such as Rep. John Conyers (D-MI) and Rep. Joe Baca (D-CA) drew attention to the discrimination against black and Latino farmers by US Department of Agriculture officials in the agency's farm lending program. Rep. Julian Dixon (D-CA) pushed for greater racial and ethnic diversity in intelligence agencies, such as the FBI and CIA. Since most black and Latino legislators were Democrats, and since they usually provided unified support for pro-minority positions on racial or ethnic issues, they were able to exert influence on the majority party.

The active and vigorous enforcement of antidiscrimination laws by the Clinton administration was protested by Republicans. Since Republican legislators were in the minority party, they could not control the agenda or stymie enforcement efforts by House Democrats. The lack of GOP influence changed after Republicans won back the Congress as a result of the 1994 midterm elections, however. In 1995 GOP leadership began to question the efforts of the Clinton administration on the civil rights front. They called hearings challenging enforcement actions by agencies such as the US Department of Justice and the US Department of Housing and Urban Development. Democrats came to the defense of the Clinton administration; black and Latino legislators in particular mounted a vigorous defense of these civil rights policies.

In this chapter, I examine the individual efforts of legislators to advocate for minority interests via the protection of civil rights. Specifically, I take a closer look at how much time members of Congress spent in committee deliberations supporting minority interests during the 103rd Congress (1993–1995), years of Democratic control of both chambers of Congress; the 104th Congress (1995–1997), years when a Republican Congress opposed a Democratic president; and the 107th Congress (2001–2003), years of continued Republican control of Congress, now under a Republican president. I argue that strategic group uplift produces systematic racial and ethnic differences between minority legislators and white legislators: black and minority legislators actively promote and defend minority interests through strategic participation in hearings. Specifically, I assess the intensity of minority legislators' commitment to minority civil rights by examining the amount of time that they spend attending and engaging in deliberations at oversight hearings in order to ensure that federal bureaucracies are pursuing policies that minorities favor. I focus on exchanges that legislators have with one another and exchanges that legislators have with federal officials and other witnesses who testify at the hearings. I pay close attention, moreover, to requests made by legislators to hold oversight hearings that pertain to minority interests, to letters or other written correspondence submitted to agency officials supporting minority positions, to the introduction of legislation that directs an agency to implement an action that minorities favor, and to testifying at congressional hearings.

In addition to examining how much time legislators spend intervening at oversight hearings (as a measure of effort and therefore intensity of commitment), I examine the substance of their interventions, focusing on whether the racial or ethnic background of legislators, a key component of strategic group uplift, leads to qualitatively different perspectives on civil rights public policy. Do they bring the same insights and rationale for supporting or opposing policies that are not favorable to minority interests? Are they effective in countering negative stereotypes about black and Latino constituents? Before addressing these questions, it is important to examine the data and methods used in this study to assess the overall responsiveness and advocacy of legislators to minority interests in oversight activity.

Measuring Advocacy of Minority Interests in Committees

There are many avenues through which legislators can conduct oversight or intervene in agency policymaking; the mechanism I test measures legislators' involvement in oversight hearings. Congressional hearings are second only to direct staff contact with a given agency as the primary means by which legislators engage in the oversight of federal agencies (Aberbach 1990). Oversight hearings allow individual members of Congress to directly question agency representatives about their efforts to implement federal policies. Quite often, legislators use this forum to criticize or praise an agency for its work in a given area (Foreman 1988; Hall and Miler 2000). The hearing can also serve as an opportunity to gather information about agency performance. Oversight hearings can be vehicles to demonstrate to constituents that the member is articulating or representing constituent viewpoints (Ogul 1976). For example, each legislative session, the House Judiciary Committee conducts hearings to examine the DOJ's enforcement of civil rights laws. Under Title VI of the Civil Rights Act of 1964, the DOJ is responsible for enforcing civil rights laws to combat discrimination in areas such as housing, employment, and public accommodations. The hearings provide a wealth of information on particular legislators' advocacy of certain policies. The transcripts detail the members and witnesses who attend the hearings and the substantive content of the deliberation among legislators and between legislators and witnesses. Additionally, they provide information on letters and questions submitted to the hearings' records.

In determining which hearings will offer insight into minority representation, it is important to note that certain topics are of particular concern to black and Latino communities. Public opinion polls show that blacks and Latinos are overwhelmingly more likely than whites to favor governmental programs such as affirmative action (Kinder and Sanders 1996; Leal 2007; Tate 1993). Blacks and Latinos are disproportionately poor and usually live in substandard housing; black Americans are more likely than whites to support strong federal government intervention to address such racial inequities (Dawson 1994, 2001). Since the end of the civil rights era, white liberals have tended to advocate more for policies that seek to address inequalities based on class rather than race, while blacks have been committed to pursuing policies that address both racial and class inequalities (Hamilton and Hamilton 1997).

Correspondingly, minority-interest policies are broadly defined in two separate policy domains: explicitly racial or ethnic policies and general social welfare policies (see appendixes A and B).[1] Explicitly racial or ethnic hearings pertain to issues such as civil rights, discrimination, racial profiling, and the enforcement of civil rights legislation. The common thread that links the racial and ethnic hearings is that they pertain to agencies' efforts to enforce or implement policies that specifically target blacks and Latinos. General social welfare hearings may include issues such as the implementation of welfare reform, review of community development block grants, domestic food distribution programs, and Medicaid. The social welfare policies may not directly target the interests of black or Latino constituents, but these policies may have a disproportionate effect on these constituents.

For example, in the 107th Congress (2001–2003), approximately sixteen explicitly racial or ethnic hearings took place from 2001 to 2002 in the House of Representatives. I coded sixof the sixteen hearings, excluding three oversight hearings that focused on funding for historically black colleges and universities because they were held at off-site locations away from Washington, DC. The difference in venue probably affected the likelihood that legislators would attend and actively participate. I randomly selected six hearings from the remaining thirteen. The remaining hearings not included in this study focused on issues such as operations oversight of the US Civil Rights Commission and racial disparities in the health care system. For the broader social welfare issues, I randomly selected ten of twenty-eight hearings. In the 103rd and 104th Congresses, I coded approximately ten hearings from each to get a representative sample.

I selected the 103rd, 104th, and 107th Congresses because they permit the examination of legislators' advocacy across different partisan configurations of government. Scholars have found that divided government, when Democrats and Republicans control separate branches of the government, can determine how much oversight takes place during any given session of Congress (Mayhew 1989; Ogul 1976). During the 103rd Congress, Democrats controlled both chambers of the Congress and the

[1]My classification of the issues dimensions is similar to the categories used by Canon (1999), "explicitly racial" and "part racial."

presidency, and in the 104th Congress Republicans gained control of the Congress while the Democrats retained control of the presidency. When government is divided, as was the case with the 104th Congress, the expectation is the Republicans will hold more oversight hearings to stymie civil rights enforcement efforts by the Democratic president.

The dependent variable, "legislators' interventions," is a proxy for the intensity of legislators' commitment to supporting black- and Latino-interest policies. The concept of legislators' interventions differs from Hall's (1996) and Gamble's (2007) concept of legislators' participation in committee activities, because the content of interventions tells us not only how often legislators participate in deliberations but also whether these legislators are for or against a policy. Consequently, considering interventions allows us to gauge if legislators' actions are consistent with the interests of blacks and Latinos. Reviewing the transcript of each hearing, I recorded the frequency and length (in number of transcript lines) of each legislator's verbal and written comments expressing distinct policy preferences consistent with minority policy interests. Other researchers have used this method (Hall 1996; Maltzman and Sigelman 1996). I assigned a value of zero to legislators who made or submitted comments that were neutral or expressed opposition to minority interests, as well as to legislators who did not make or submit comments. The criteria used to assess the valence of legislators' comments are explained in appendix C.

I pooled the intervention data for all individual legislators across committees to create a single sample for each policy dimension. Verbal and written intervention data for individual legislators at the House Government Reform Committee hearing regarding racial profiling, for example, were combined with data for individual legislators at the House Financial Services Committee subcommittee hearing relating to enforcement of fair housing laws. It was necessary to pool the data because no single committee held enough racial/ethnic or social welfare oversight hearings to support multivariate analyses of the various hypotheses. I used the same method to construct the sample for the social welfare hearings, discussed in chapter 5.

Finally, I conducted the analysis on several levels. I broke the intervention data into two groups, one of those legislators who served on the committees responsible for conducting the specific hearing and another of legislators who were not assigned to the committee, and I analyzed each group to determine whether black and Latino legislators differed in their advocacy of black and Latino interests from white legislators who participated in the hearings. As I demonstrate in the following section, the committees under consideration are more racially, ethnically, and ideologically diverse than the full House. White legislators on the House Financial Services Committee, for instance, are just as liberal as black and Latino legislators on this committee, and we should therefore expect them to be just as active on racial and social welfare issues. In other words, this committee is filled with preference outliers, as are others like it; in consequence, it may be difficult to perceive any race- or ethnic-based differences in committee members' behavior. The second analysis, of intervention by noncommittee members who engaged in committee deliberations, either as witnesses or as guests of the committee, or who submitted written statements for the record, allows me to examine those legislators who decide to engage in advocacy through legislative intervention even though they are not part of the committee or subcommittee holding a hearing.

Because interventions involve the number of transcript lines attributed to legislators who participated in oversight activity, I chose the zero-inflated negative binomial (ZINB) model to estimate the intensity of legislator intervention for stronger enforcement of civil rights and implementation of minority-interest social welfare policies. The ZINB model fits these data because of the overdispersion and excess number of zeros in the sample. Overdispersion occurs when the conditional variance exceeds the conditional mean. The distribution of interventions for stronger enforcement or implementation of policies is uneven when legislators who engaged in the oversight activity participated often and spent a significant amount of time advocating their positions compared with legislators who did not participate at all. The dispersion could result from such factors as race, ethnicity, leadership position, partisanship, or unobserved heterogeneity.

The ZINB model is preferable to negative binomial regression because it accounts for the differences in the probability distributions and the large cluster of zeros. Whereas negative binomial regression would assume that every legislator has a positive probability distribution of intervening in favor of stronger civil rights enforcement or implementation of social welfare policies, the underlying logic of the ZINB model is that the processes that produce zeros in the observations may come from two different probability distributions. First, some zero observations are produced by legislators who do not participate in any oversight activity. Nonparticipation by these legislators inflates the number of zeros when we examine the likelihood of legislators' being in favor of minority-interest policies. Second, a process produces zeros for (a) legislators who attended or wrote letters that were either against or neutral toward stronger civil rights enforcement or stronger implementation of social welfare hearings and (b) legislators who attended hearings but did not say anything. The ZINB goes one step further than the negative binomial: it allows the estimation of these mixed observations from possibly different probability distributions, accounting for the zeros by increasing the conditional variance and changing the conditional mean to the probability of the zero counts (Long and Freese 2003).

In models that follow in chapers 4 and 5, I used a variety of control variables that are included in standard models of legislators' vote choice and legislative participation (see chapter 2 for a detailed explanation of the variables). The variable Percent Black Voting-Age Population and the Percent Hispanic Voting-Age Population in members' districts are used to assess constituent influence. To assess electoral safety of the district, I used the percentage of votes that the legislator received in general election of the respective year—for this study, 1992, 1994, and 2000. Other standard controls include partisan affiliation of the legislator party, where Democrat is coded as 1 and Republican as 0; region (South/North), where South is coded as 1 and all other regions as 0; and district class interests (Median Family Income). Legislators who hold institutional positions of power on a committee, such as committee chairs or members with ranking minority status, have more resources to engage in oversight than do members who do not hold such positions.

Racial and Ethnic Diversity of Congressional Overseers and Legislative Responsiveness

Congress has become more ideologically liberal as it has grown more racially and ethnically diverse. The greatest change in membership has occurred primarily in the US House of Representatives, however. Figure 4.1 shows that between 1951 and 2004, the representation of racial and ethnic minority members in the House grew from 1 to 15 percent, while racial and ethnic diversity in the Senate increased only a fraction, from 1 to 3 percent. Specifically, in 1971, when the Congressional Black Caucus was founded, only thirteen blacks served in the House of Representatives, compared to thirty-nine in 2001. In 1976, when the Congressional Hispanic Caucus was first organized, only five Latinos served in the House, compared to nineteen in 2001. Correspondingly, the racial and ethnic composition of congressional committees has become more diverse, which is important because many minority-interest issues, such as racial profiling and fair housing enforcement, are dealt with in these committees and in their subcommittees. For example, the House Financial Services' Subcommittee on Housing and Community Opportunity plays a vital role in overseeing the fair housing enforcement efforts of the Department of Housing and Urban Development (HUD). Likewise, the House Judiciary's Subcommittee on the Constitution is one of the many committees that oversee the operations of the Department of Justice's Division on Civil Rights.

The legislators who serve on House committees are not randomly selected. Legislators try to get appointed to committees so they can provide benefits to their constituents. Legislators who represent districts with large cities, such as New York and Chicago, are more likely to serve on commit-

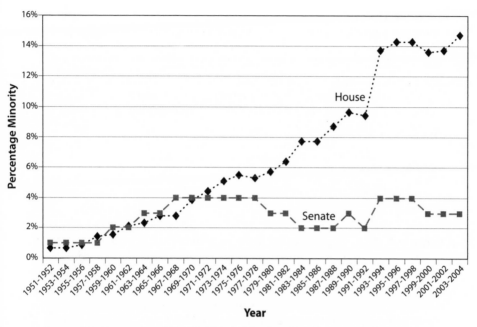

FIGURE 4.1 Congressional Racial/Ethnic Membership Diversity, 1951–2004

tees that address urban issues, including banking and finance, such as the House Financial Services Committee, than they are to serve on a committee such as the House Agriculture Committee, which has jurisdiction over many rural and agricultural issues. Thus, committees and their subcommittees are composed mainly of legislators who have specific preferences for policies that affect their particular district (Hall and Evans 1990; Hall and Grofman 1990).

These expectations turn out to be correct. Although the number of black representatives in the three Congresses analyzed herein approached the proportion of black people in the general US population, black legislators were overrepresented on the committees in the sample. Table 4.1 shows that for the 107th Congress (2001–2002), black legislators represented 14 percent of the committee sample, compared to only 9 percent in the full House. Latino legislators represented 5 percent of the committee sample, compared to 4 percent in the full House. Among Latino subgroup members, Puerto Rican legislators were more likely to be members of the committees than Mexican American and Cuban American legislators. Puerto Rican legislators comprised 55 percent of the Latino delegation in the sample, while they represented only 19 percent of the Latino total

TABLE 4.1
Racial and Ethnic Composition of Committee Sample versus Full House
Composition[*]

	Committee Sample			Full House[*]
	103rd Congress (1993–1995)	104th Congress (1995–1997)	107th Congress (2001–2003)	
White	73%	85%	79%	87%
Black	22%	11%	14%	9%
Latino	5%	5%	5%	4%

*Full House composition is the same for each Congress.

delegation in the House. Puerto Rican legislators such as Nydia Velazquez
(D-NY), Jose Serrano (D-NJ), and Luis Gutiérrez (D-IL) are primarily
from urban areas in the Northeast and Illinois. Mexican American legislators, who are the majority of the Latino delegation in the House, are underrepresented on the committees that are most likely to conduct civil
rights or racial/ethnic hearings. They represent 80 percent of the legislators in the Latino House delegation but make up only 22 percent of the
Latino legislators on the committees in the sample. California Democrats
such as Xavier Becerra and Joe Baca provide the main Mexican American
representation on committees dealing with civil rights or racial/ethnic issues.

Not only are these committees more racially and ethnically diverse than
the full House, but the minority legislators who are on these committees
are considerably more liberal than the full House. To get a general assess-
ment of whether the committees contained in my sample contain "preference outliers," I use Poole and Rosenthal DW-NOMINATE scores as a
measure of a member's ideological disposition. The first dimension of the
Poole and Rosenthal score reflects legislators' roll-call voting behavior on
general and social economic policies. The score is on a scale from 1 to –1,
where a 1 is conservative and a –1 is liberal. Table 4.2 shows that, as expected, black and Latino legislators in the sample of committee members
were more liberal than the House average for each group. Only in the
107th Congress were Latino committee members more conservative than
their House average. Latino legislators' ideology scores are more conservative because of the inclusion of Latino Republicans, who are more conservative than Latino Democrats. Since almost all blacks in the Congress
are Democrats—with the exception of J. C. Watts (R-OK) and Gary Franks
(R-CT) in the 103rd and 104th Congresses respectively—the relevant point
of comparison is with other Democrats. Surprisingly, only in the 103rd
Congress were white committee members more liberal than white members
in the full House. The reason for more conservative white committee mem-

TABLE 4.2
Committee Members' Ideology Scores versus Full House Ideology Scores

	103rd Congress Committee	*103rd Congress Full House*	*104th Congress Committee*	*104th Congress Full House*	*107th Congress Committee*	*107th Congress Full House*
Black	−.59	−.55	−.60	−.50	−.57	−.51
Latino	−.58	−.31	−.42	−.26	−.25	−.27
White	−.01	.01	.17	.12	.17	.13

Source: DW-NOMINATE First Dimension Scores: http://www.voteview.com

bers reflects the Republican takeover of Congress and these conservative members electing to serve on committees to implement a conservative agenda.

The increase in black and Latino members on congressional committees has prompted a corresponding increase in the percentage of hearings devoted to racial and ethnic issues. Figure 4.2 shows the level of attention paid to explicitly racial or ethnic issues from 1991 through 2003. The number of hearings in general devoted to racial or ethnic issues correlates with which party controls the House and the presidency. The greatest attention was paid to racial and ethnic issues in hearings during 1993–1994, when Democrats controlled the presidency and the House. Generally, more hearings that focus on racial or ethnic issues are held when Democrats control the Congress, regardless of who holds the executive. Issues such as civil rights enforcement are part of the liberal agenda that is most associated with constituents of the Democratic Party. Since black and Latino legislators are primarily Democrats, their ability to get their requests for hearings granted is naturally greater when Congress is under Democratic control than when it is under Republican control. The attention devoted to racial and ethnic issues decreased dramatically as a result of the Republican takeover of the House and Senate in 1994. It remained low under GOP control compared to Democratic control and dropped even lower when Republicans gained control of the presidency in 2000. The level of attention to racial or ethnic issues increased again when Democrats regained control of the House after the 2006 midterm elections.

Civil Rights Enforcement in the Clinton Years

In 1992 the Democrats regained control of the presidency and maintained control of Congress. President Bill Clinton promised to be more vigorous in enforcing many of the civil rights laws, especially as they related to racial or ethnic discrimination. His commitment was greeted with skepticism by many civil rights organizations when the administration withdrew the

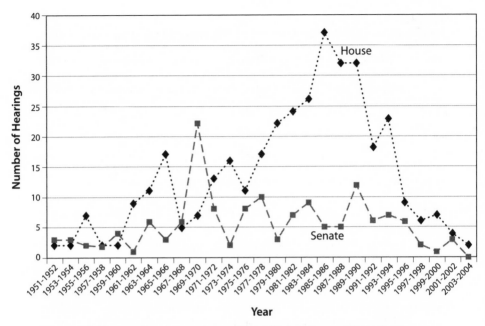

FIGURE 4.2 Congressional Attention to Racial/Ethnic Issues, 1951–2004

nomination of Harvard University law professor Lani Guinier as head of the civil rights division of the US Department of Justice. Guinier would have been the first African American woman to head the division. She had the support of the NAACP and the Congressional Black Caucus, but Republicans strongly objected to her legal writings pertaining to electoral voting procedures. Clinton later nominated civil rights attorney Deval Patrick to head the civil rights division at the Department of Justice. Patrick had a record of being a strong defender of civil rights and was subsequently confirmed by the Senate. He eventually gained the confidence of congressional Democrats, and thus the level of intervention by the Democratic Congress was held to a minimum.

The election not only brought a return of unified Democratic government but also ushered in the largest contingent of African Americans and Latinos ever elected to serve in any one Congress. The increase in the number of African American and Latino legislators can largely be traced to the redistricting efforts that occurred in many southern and southwestern states. The infusion of African Americans into Congress resulted in greater attention by individual legislators to minority interests in terms of bill sponsorship, voting, committee markups, and obtaining federal dollars for their districts (Canon 1999; Gamble 2007; Grose 2003; Hall 1996; Sinclair-Chapman 2003). Table 4.3 shows the multivariate results, which

TABLE 4.3

Interventions by Members of Congress for Stronger Enforcement of Civil Rights Policies in the 103rd Congress (1993–1995)

Explanatory Variables	Committee Members	Committee and Noncommittee Members
Party	1.04[+]	1.03[**]
	(.75)	(.30)
Black	.01	.07
	(.65)	(.44)
Latino	−1.32	−.85
	(.79)	(.65)
Chair	1.27[**]	1.20[**]
	(.23)	(.25)
Ranking minority member	.56	.38
	(.90)	(.33)
% black voting-age population	−.01	−.01
	(.02)	(.01)
% Hispanic voting-age population	.02[+]	.01
	(.01)	(.01)
Median family income	−.04[*]	−.03[+]
	(.02)	(.02)
South	−.84	−.45[+]
	(.35)	(.29)
Electoral safety	.03	.03[**]
	(.03)	(.01)
Member of assigned committee	—	−.37
		(.23)
Constant	2.42[**]	2.14[**]
	(1.07)	(.92)
Log pseudo-likelihood	−234.57	−299.87
Wald chi-square (10)	460.74	146.48
	(p<.001)	(p<.001)
Alpha	.35	.34
	(.23)	(.19)
N	123	138

Robust standard errors are in parentheses.

[*]Statistically significant at .05 level, one-tailed test.

[**]Statistically significant at .01 level, one-tailed test.

[+]Statistically significant at .10 level, one-tailed test.

reveal how much time legislators devote to advocacy for minority interests.[2] Despite the increase in racial and ethnic diversity on congressional
committees, however, there were no significant differences between black,
Latino, and white legislators in their level of advocacy for stronger civil
rights enforcement. As table 4.3 indicates, the strongest predictor of legislators' intervention on behalf of blacks and Latinos was party affiliation.
Democrats—black, white, and Latino—spent roughly equal amounts of
time advocating for stronger enforcement of civil rights at the various
committees. The fact that fellow Democrat Bill Clinton was president explains why black and Latino legislators did not feel a need to intervene to
a greater degree and why the level of congressional intervention was low
compared to Republican-controlled Congresses. The Department of Justice under the Clinton administration included well-known civil rights advocates such as Deval Patrick, the director of the Civil Rights Division.
Since the Clinton administration was on the same page as many black and
Latino legislators, minority legislators made the strategic decision to focus
their advocacy efforts in other areas where they believed the Clinton administration did not share their views. Table 4.4 further demonstrates this
point by showing the predicted number of lines that legislators dedicated
toward advocacy of minority interests. The predicted line counts in the table
demonstrate the amount of time legislators devoted to speaking at the
hearing, questioning witnesses, or testifying in favor of minority-interest
policies. Legislators who spent the most time intervening or engaged in
the deliberations will have more lines, while those who did not will have
fewer lines. Committee Democrats devoted 39 lines to advocating for
stronger enforcement of civil rights policies, compared to 15 lines for Republicans on the committee. When both committee members and non-
commitee members who intervened at the hearings are considered, Democrats' level of intervention increased to 58 lines and the Republican level
dropped to 6 lines.

Return to Republican Rule and the Fight for Minority Rights

Disenchanted with various corruption scandals that plagued congressional
Democrats, voters returned control of the Congress to Republicans in
1994. Republicans promised to restore public confidence in government
and to reduce the size of government and the federal budget. Democrats,
in addition to losing control of the Senate, lost control of the House of
Representatives for the first time since 1952 and only the third time in

[2] For simplicity, the ZINB results that follow in tables 4.3, 4.5, 4.6, 5.4, 5.5, and 5.6 present the second stage of legislators' interventions for civil rights and social welfare. The associated first stage for these models can be found in appendixes E through J.

TABLE 4.4

Intervention Levels for Stronger Civil Rights Enforcement by
Political Party in the 103rd Congress (1993–1995)

	Committee	Committee and Noncommittee
Democrats	39	58
Republicans	15	6

sixty-two years. The role of minority legislators in the 104th Congress is in sharp contrast to their role in the Democrat-controlled 103rd Congress. Since the majority of black and Latino legislators were Democrats, the gains that many black and Latino legislators had achieved in leadership positions were lost. Charles Rangel, John Conyers, Matthew Martínez, and Henry B. González, for instance, lost valuable committee chairmanships. As members of the minority party, their influence decreased. Democrats' removal from power meant that they lost the ability to control the legislative agenda. They could not control which bills received a committee hearing or the nature of agency oversight, nor could they ensure that oversight hearings would be friendly toward minority interests.

When Republicans took control of Congress, they introduced bills that sought to eliminate or diminish many existing civil rights laws and programs; one bill, for example, sought to repeal bilingual voting requirements that required election officials to provide election and campaign materials in a language other than English. Committee chairs conducted oversight hearings aimed at scaling back the use of affirmative action programs in government employment and contracting. The character of these committee hearings was remarkably different from the previous Democratically controlled congress. Democrats who were supportive of Clinton officials at the Department of Justice were now defending the administration against a Republican assault on policies designed to address racial inequalities in society. Democrats in general fought against efforts to eliminate bilingual ballots and affirmative action, but it was black legislators and Latino leaders who lived in predominately Hispanic districts who were most active in defending these programs.

The multivariate results from the zero-inflated negative binomial in table 4.5 confirm that black committee members, Latino committee leaders, and members with a significant Latino presence in their districts were likely to spend more time intervening in civil rights policies than white legislators in this Congress. Black legislators spent more time than their Latino or white peers defending the continuance of policies to promote diversity in the workplace by supporting programs such as affirmative action and stronger enforcement of equal employment opportunity laws. The second column in the table shows that black legislators and Democrats who were not assigned

TABLE 4.5

Interventions by Members of Congress for Stronger Enforcement of Civil Rights Policies in the 104th Congress (1995–1997)

Explanatory Variables	Committee Members	Committee and Noncommittee Members
Party	.80**	1.08**
	(.23)	(.24)
Black	.95**	.83**
	(.24)	(.30)
Latino	−2.74	−.53
	(.43)	(.37)
Chair	.15	.18
	(.48)	(.46)
Ranking minority member	.83**	.56*
	(.33)	(.27)
Latino ranking minority member	1.45**	−.22
	(.42)	(.56)
% black voting-age population	−.02	−.02
	(.01)	(.01)
% Hispanic voting-age population	.02+	.01
	(.01)	(.01)
Median family income	−.04	−.06**
	(.03)	(.02)
South	−.39+	−.40+
	(.27)	(.25)
Electoral safety	.01*	.01*
	(.01)	(.01)
Member of assigned committee	—	.72**
		(.29)
Constant	4.35**	3.92**
	(.97)	(.73)
Log pseudo-likelihood	−227.95	−328.35
Wald chi-square (11)	297.12	65.21
	(p<.001)	(p<.001)
Alpha	.19	.28
	(.22)	(.16)
N	130	163

Robust standard errors are in parentheses.
*Statistically significant at .05 level, one-tailed test.
**Statistically significant at .01 level, one-tailed test.
+Statistically significant at .10 level, one-tailed test.

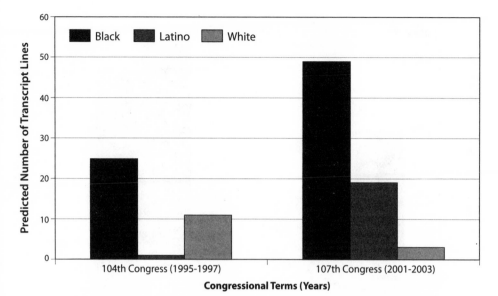

FIGURE 4.3 Intervention Levels by Committee Members for Stronger Civil Rights Enforcement by Race/Ethnicity

to the committees were also more likely to intervene on behalf of minority interests than white legislators not on the committee.

Figure 4.3 shows that the predicted rate of total transcript lines for black legislators exceeded that of white and Latino legislators for committee members. Black legislators devoted 25 lines to advocating for minority interests, compared to 11 lines for white legislators and 1 line for Latino legislators. Legislators with the most lines are those legislators who spent the most time engaging in committee deliberations or submitting written statements for the stronger enforcement of civil rights or explicitly racial/ethnic policies that benefit black and Latino constituents. Figure 4.4 shows that when examining all legislators who participated at the hearing, black legislators still intervened at a higher rate with 21 lines compared to 10 for white legislators. Latino legislators also contributed 10 lines.

Black legislators pressed federal officials to devote more time to ensuring that federal agencies such as the Central Intelligence Agency and Federal Bureau of Investigation were racially and ethnically diverse and ensuring that affirmative action programs in business and employment were not eliminated. One such effort took place in a hearing held by the Subcommittee on Employer-Employee Relations of the House Committee on Economic and Educational Opportunities. The hearing focused in part on President Clinton's federal review of programs relating to affirmative action.

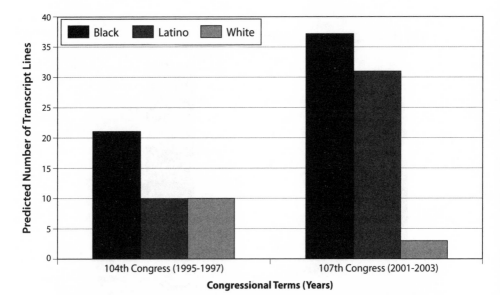

FIGURE 4.4 Intervention Levels by Committee and Noncommittee Members for Stronger Civil Rights Enforcement by Race/Ethnicity

In the hearing, Assistant Attorney General Deval Patrick testified to legislators that the administration's review of affirmative action did not signal a lack of commitment to these programs. He emphasized the administration's commitment "to the goal of expanding opportunity for all Americans in education, in employment, and in the economy generally" and emphasized that "regrettably discrimination on the basis of race or of gender or of ethnicity persists in this country . . . real life, pernicious discrimination of the here and now" (*Hearings on Affirmative Action in Employment*, 36). However, the Republican chair of the committee, Harris Fawell (R-IL), explained the rationale for the hearing in terms that emphasized his party's critique of affirmative action. He was concerned that affirmative action programs discriminated against whites and questioned whether affirmative action was a useful tool for integrating societal institutions: "Affirmative action has brought us real achievements. But now, 17 years after the Bakke decision, we should ask if it is time to consider whether we have passed that period of 'transitional inequality' and should begin to move away from our reliance on affirmative action, and . . . we should also ask what alternatives are there other than the specific remedies of the various civil rights acts to further address racial and gender discrimination" (31).

In the context of this suggestion that affirmative action should be dismantled, black legislators such as representatives Major Owens (D-NY), Donald Payne (D-NJ), and William Clay Sr. (D-MO) strongly defended the use of affirmative action programs and voiced skepticism regarding the

GOP leadership's rationale for conducting the hearings. They believed the hearing was an attempt by Republicans to roll back the gains achieved by racial and ethnic minorities. Clay stated: "Today's hearing is designed to begin the process of returning the gatekeepers the mean prerogative of keeping the gates closed to those who traditionally have been denied equal opportunity; minorities and women. The efforts to repeal, reverse, or eliminate affirmative action are not remotely related to the vulgar argument that unqualified women and unqualified blacks are taking jobs that should go to qualified white men" (32). He concluded by saying that affirmative action must be defended: "There is no widespread abuse of affirmative action programs in employment. On the contrary, ongoing affirmative action programs have produced significant improvements in occupational positions of women and minorities, but have not closed the gap disparity. Therefore, any effort to weaken, modify, reverse, or eliminate efforts to address these historical injustices must be vigorously opposed on every front" (33).

In addition to support for affirmative action by black legislators, Latino leaders, and not Latino rank-and-file members, spent a significant amount of time intervening for minority interests (see table 4.5). Latino ranking minority members spent more time advocating for stronger enforcement of civil rights laws, at 241 lines, than did white ranking minority members, at 57 lines. An example of this commitment is demonstrated by the subcommittee's ranking committee member, Matthew Martínez (D-CA), devoted considerable time to defending the use of affirmative action programs:

> When I was a kid, I went to school in a neighborhood that was 78 percent Hispanic. Sixty-eight percent of the school population was Hispanic. There was not one Hispanic teacher, as a result no role model, and I will tell you why. Nobody was even thinking about going into that profession because they looked around and they say "They would not hire us anyway," and that was the truth. For many years, people of minority were not hired for particular kinds of industries, and why? Because the people who headed those industries and made those decisions felt that it would not be proper to put somebody of a minority in front of a class or as a supervisor on a job because customers would not come in and do business. I know a friend who denied, after he was in World War II ace fighter pilot, who was denied working for the airlines simply because he was Hispanic, and it would not look good to see a Hispanic get into the cockpit. (85)

Latino legislators also advocated for opportunities for minority-owned businesses. Nydia Velazquez (D-NY), the ranking Democrat on the Subcommittee on Regulation and Paperwork for the House Committee on Small Business, strongly defended minority businesses and efforts to create opportunities for minority businesses: "Let me say at the onset that I have always been a very strong supporter of minority small businesses. I believe in granting the minority entrepreneurs of our era both the opportunities that they deserve and the help that they need. Because of this I have been and will continue to be an outspoken advocate of the 8A and other minority set-aside programs" (*Regulatory Barriers to Minority Entrepreneurs*, 2–3). The subcommittee hearing at which she testified focused on how federal and state regulations impact minority small business. Velazquez was arguing against Republicans such as the chairman of the subcommittee, Rep. James Talent (R-MO), who believed that federal regulations protecting small business should be repealed. In defending the Davis-Bacon Act, which requires federal construction projects to pay prevailing wages to workers, Velazquez argued:

> I understand that much of the testimony today focuses on the repeal of the Davis-Bacon Act. While I respect the views of the panelists, I take strong exception to any attempt to undo that statute and subvert the purposes that it serves. Repeal of Davis-Bacon, like the abandonment of the minimum wage, suggests competition based upon the lowest wages and the most minimal living standards. It is a wage race to the bottom, with contracts going to the bidder with the most desperate labor force. The elimination of Davis-Bacon merely opens opportunity for workers to join the ranks of the working poor. It certainly won't help minority individuals and families to ever own their own home or send their children to college. (2–3)

In this hearing, Velazquez's views were opposed by Floyd Flake (D-NY), a member of the CBC, who favored reducing regulatory burdens and lowering the capital gains tax to help minority businesses. In espousing this view, Flake opposed the CBC and NAACP, which argued these measures would not do much to eliminate poverty or help minority businesses. Velazquez used the example of the failure of Operation Bootstrap in Puerto Rico to criticize Flake's viewpoint, as well as that of Jack Kemp, the secretary of HUD:

> [Kemp] mentioned that Luis Munoz Marin, former governor of Puerto Rico, he was the person in charge of creating an economic model for Puerto Rico for industrialization known as Operation Bootstrap. It happened to be that Puerto Rico has the highest unemployment rate in the Nation, close to 30 percent. Yet, American corporations are doing business in Puerto Rico. They get tax incentives; and for jobs creation, they get $70,000 for job creation. It seems like former Governor Luis Munoz' economic model did not work in Puerto Rico. It has not worked, and it will never work. They are making the money and running away with the profits. They are not reinvesting in Puerto Rico. That is at the center of

Mr. Kemp's and Mr. Flake's testimony today. What they said is that the main problem for minority entrepreneurs is lack of access to capital. (20)

Minority legislators also worked to ensure that antidiscrimination laws in employment were enforced. Equal Employment Opportunity laws were difficult to enforce under a Republican-controlled Congress. Republicans did not increase the funding for the Equal Employment Opportunity Commission, even as the number of cases continued to rise. In one hearing relating to reviewing the EEOC's efforts to resolve discrimination cases, the chair of the Subcommittee on Employer-Employee Relations for the House Committee on Economic and Educational Opportunities, Rep. Harris Fawell (R-IL), expressed dismay at the backlog in the processing of discrimination complaints. Although the chairman voiced sentiments that were sympathetic to minority interests, he did not forcefully advocate for greater funding or more staff. The Clinton administration officials and black and Latino legislators argued that greater resources were necessary to help resolve the increased caseload. Matthew Martínez (D-CA), the ranking Democrat on the subcommittee, emphasized this point: "One thing that you did not mention, Mr. Chairman—and I wish you had—is that with the increased load, there has been decreased funding. Therein lies a lot of the problem. The caseload—you did mention—of each individual worker at EEOC has increased dramatically" (*Hearing on Equal Employment Opportunity Commission (EEOC) Administrative Reforms/ Case Processing*, 2–3).

Black legislators also spent time defending positions normally more salient to Latinos than to blacks. For example, before the Subcommittee on Early Childhood, Youth and Families of the Committee on Economic and Educational Opportunities they fought against bills aimed at establishing English as the official language for all government documents. Shelia Jackson-Lee (D-TX) attacked the GOP proposal to make English the official language of government: "Legislation which would establish English as a national language runs counter to our nation's history and would create a new and unprecedented role for the federal government," Jackson-Lee argued. "The Founders of this country recognized the danger of restricting its citizens' freedom of expression. Language, like religion, is an intensely personal form of self-expression which must not be subject to governmental regulation" (*Hearing on English as ta Common Language*, 51–52).

The percentage of Hispanics residing in a congressional district plays a significant role in determining the level of legislators' intervention on behalf of minority interests. The larger the share of Latinos in a congressional district, the more time that district's legislators will spend intervening for stronger civil rights enforcement. In oversight hearings addressing the lack of diversity in the US intelligence agencies, Rep. Ronald Coleman (D-TX), a white Democrat from the El Paso area who represented a majority-Hispanic district, spent a significant portion of his time defending minority interests. As in remarks that he made before the House Permanent Select Committee on Intelligence regarding diversity of staffing in the intelligence agencies: "If the intelligence community is to remain competitive in the future," he noted, "efforts to recruit and retain individuals from all segments of our society must be institutionalized within personnel practices. I hope our witnesses will address ongoing as well as new initiatives that have been implemented that address the underrepresentation of minorities, women, and handicapped persons" (*Human Resource and Diversity*, 3).

Diversity of Perspectives

Strategic group uplift motivates legislators to be active in their advocacy for minority interests and brings perspectives to deliberations that nonminority legislators do not have. Through actions such as testifying at hearings, Latino legislators who are not on a given committee provide a different perspective to deliberations than do members who are on the committee. Moreover, legislators may request from the chair that they be allowed to engage in the questioning of witnesses, as did Jose Serrano (D-NY) and Ed Pastor (D-AZ) in a hearing relating to establishing English as a common language. To take another example, in a hearing before the House Committee on the Judiciary congressional Democrats fought against efforts by Republicans to repeal bilingual voting provisions of the Voting Rights Act. The bill under discussion would have done away with the requirement that ballots and campaign materials had to be provided in English and another language. The Republicans argued that bilingual ballots were a waste of time and did very little to stimulate political participation by citizens. Rep. Bob Goodlatte (R-VA) made this point, for example, when he argued: "Government mandated bilingualism does not work. It may be designated to be inclusive, but in reality it is separatist in nature. It would create two neighboring separate but equal cultures, and it would begin to eat at the fabric of what makes us Americans unique in our diversity. Bilingual ballots do not increase voting participation by language minorities, nor do they guarantee, as the proponents have argued, the ability to cast an independent informed vote (*Bilingual Voting Requirements Repeal Act*, 1). The Department of Justice, represented by the head of the Civil Rights Division, Deval Patrick, opposed the passage of the bill. At the hearing, Reps. Nydia Velazquez (D-CA) and Xavier Becerra (D-CA) testified against the bill, claiming that it would take away gains made by language minorities, and they supported efforts to maintain the bilingual requirements. Velazquez made an eloquent argument against the bill:

We have to tear down these barriers, not erect new ones. Encouraging people to register and vote is very close to my heart. I have spent much of my life in the Latino community registering voters. While still in Puerto Rico, I learned about the huge disparity between voter turnout on the island and on the mainland. By launching the most comprehensive voter registration campaign among Puerto Ricans in this country, I was able to register 250,000 in 3 years. I was able to increase voter participation from 36 percent to 52 percent. All people needed was the opportunity and understanding. Otherwise, they will not vote. Our job here in Congress is clear. We must provide the tools and encouragement new voters need. We must safeguard multilingual ballots. (12)

Although on average, black and Latino legislators differ in terms of their background and experiences from white legislators, some white legislators bring perspectives to the table that are closely related to the backgrounds of racial and ethnic minorities. For example, Barney Frank, a white Democrat from Massachusetts and ranking Democrat on the Subcommittee on the Constitution, strongly opposes efforts to eliminate bilingual voting information and ballots. Frank's experience of participating in the civil rights movement Freedom Rides contributed to his opposition to the repeal of bilingual voting requirements: "I was there in the summer of 1964 when blacks still could not vote in Mississippi, except at peril of their life," he said (*Bilingual Voting Requirements Repeal Act*, 59). This experience informed his view of the bill under discussion. Frank noted that the bilingual voting requirements were particularly helpful to "older people who have become citizens who are not fully comfortable yet in English," not for younger people. He noted: "You get older people, particularly when we have complicated referenda questions, why anyone gets so exercised about the fact that we've got some 70-year-old read a referendum question in his or her native language baffles me. I don't think there's a logical argument for it" (59).

Eliot Engel's personal experience similarly shaped his advocacy in oversight hearings against English-only proposals. Engel is a white Democrat from New York. He referred to the fact that his grandparents did not know English when they came to the United States before World War I. Engel said his grandparents, as well as others, learned English without any official language requirements. He did not believe a law was needed to encourage it. Additionally, his experience as a teacher in a bilingual school in the South Bronx also affected his perspective:

I think it [bilingualism] has worked pretty well, quite frankly, and before I became an elected official and before I got my law degree, I was a teacher in a bilingual school in the South Bronx, in fact, in Mr. Serrano's district. Mr. Serrano and I represent the Bronx. I taught typing in those days 25 years ago, and I taught it bilingually. I am not that good in Spanish, but I can get by, and I did not think that it put students at a disadvantage. I think it actually helped the students. The purpose of bilingualism to me is not to perpetuate the old language, but it is to teach children in the old language so they can help learn the new language even better (*Hearing on English as a Common Language*, 36–37).

In two hearings on the use of English as a common language, Republicans were critical of bilingual education programs, while Democrats were generally supporters. In the 103rd Congress, when Democrats controlled the House, they sought to pass legislation that provided more funding and federal resources for bilingual education programs. When the Republicans took control of the House after the 1994 elections, congressional language hearings focused more on passing laws establishing English as the official language of the United States and reducing funding and support for bilingual education programs. Although black, white, and Latino Democrats were supportive of bilingual education, they brought distinct perspectives to the deliberations. Latino legislators, regardless of their subgroup, provided a perspective directly related to being a member of the Latino ethnic group. They provided that voice throughout the congressional deliberations, even when their level of advocacy was not, statistically speaking, different from that of whites. While white legislators, especially white Democrats, can advocate effectively on behalf of minority interests, and while their personal experiences helped shape their perspectives and outlook on the issues under discussion, black and Latino legislators tend to provide and share a point of view that comes from being part of the minority group and having experiences and insights that only being a group member can provide.

Civil Rights Enforcement in the Post-9/11 Era

The 2000 election of George W. Bush returned control of the presidency to the Republican Party. Not only did the GOP control the executive branch, but the party also controlled the House and Senate. President Bush immediately started to scale back the efforts of the Clinton Administration relating to civil rights enforcement. The Department of Justice reduced the number of class-action lawsuits against businesses that discriminated against minorities and in employment. Along with the Republican Congress, it supported efforts aimed at limiting affirmative action and bilingual education programs. The devastating 2001 attacks on the World Trade Center and Pentagon took place in this context. Subsequently, the focus on national security and stemming the tide of terrorist attacks on the US homeland dominated the legislative agenda. However, the Congress still maintained a focus on many racial or ethnic issues. The committees continued to oversee such matters as civil rights enforcement by the Department of Justice. Black and Latino legislators were more likely to attend these hearings than white legislators, and they were more likely to spend more time intervening on behalf of the interests of black and Latino constituents.

Black and Latino legislators spent a significant amount of time at the hearings directing comments at agency and local officials calling for stronger enforcement of antidiscrimination laws in housing and employment. Specifically, either they asked Congress to dedicate more resources to agency enforcement efforts or they were critical of the inaction of agency officials in responding to previous congressional requests to replace or remove agency personnel. Table 4.6 shows that black, Latino, and white legislators differed substantially in the intensity of their advocacy of stronger enforcement and their support for racial policies that benefit blacks and Latinos.

The insignificance of party in the 107th Congress may demonstrate differences in issue priorities among legislators and may not necessarily reflect a lack of Democratic support for racial or ethnic policies. As mentioned earlier, legislators have limited time and resources and cannot attend to all issues (Bauer, Pool, and Dexter 1963; Hall 1996). In the post-9/11 context, black and Latino Democrats, because of racial or ethnic group consciousness, may have been more willing than whites to place a priority on racial/ethnic group-specific issues.

HUD and the DOJ are responsible for enforcing the antidiscrimination provisions of the 1968 Fair Housing Act. HUD is charged with processing housing discrimination complaints and referring violations that require litigation to the Department of Justice. Like the EEOC, HUD is underfunded and lacks the resources to resolve the many cases that come to it. Many hearings in the 107th Congress focused on housing discrimination complaints and the inability of the agency to resolve them. One such hearing, a joint hearing of the House Financial Services Subcommittee on Housing and Community Opportunity and its Subcommittee on Oversight and Investigations, involved an examination of HUD's efforts to enforce housing laws designed to stop discrimination against minorities and the disabled. This hearing preceded hearings relating to the Fair Housing Bill sponsored by subcommittee chair Rep. Marge Roukema (R-NY). Consistent with the quantitative results, the testimony revealed distinct differences along racial and ethnic lines. Most of the participation and comments directed at HUD officials calling for stronger enforcement of fair housing laws came from black and Latino legislators. The main difference between blacks, Latinos, and whites was that most minority legislators called for more resources to be dedicated to enforcing civil rights legisla-

TABLE 4.6

Interventions by Members of Congress for Stronger Enforcement of Civil Rights Policies in the 107th Congress (2001–2003)

Explanatory Variables	Committee Members	Committee and Noncommittee Members
Party	−.26	.06
	(.42)	(.36)
Black	1.14*	.57**
	(.54)	(.23)
Latino	1.40**	1.81**
	(.53)	(.43)
Chair	.55	.69
	(.43)	(.51)
Ranking minority member	.42	.41
	(.41)	(.39)
Black ranking minority member	2.98**	2.49**
	(.59)	(.53)
% black voting-age population	.32	1.65**
	(1.11)	(.72)
% Hispanic voting-age population	−.15	−.04
	(.74)	(.66)
Median family income	.02	.02**
	(.01)	(.01)
South	−1.59**	−1.23**
	(.33)	(.30)
Electoral safety	.01	−.002
	(.01)	(.01)
Member of assigned committee	—	−.34*
		(.20)
Constant	1.62+	2.74**
	(1.13)	(1.14)
Log pseudo-likelihood	−256.31	−318.05
Wald chi-square (11)	131.62	145.15
	(p<.01)	(p<.01)
Alpha	.30	−1.22
	(.19)	(.52)
N	174	192

Robust standard errors are in parentheses.
*Statistically significant at .05 level, one-tailed test.
**Statistically significant at .01 level, one-tailed test.
+Statistically significant at .10 level, one-tailed test.

tion and for greater effort by the agency in general; Rep. Luis Gutiérrez (D-IL), for instance, argued that strict enforcement of fair housing laws was necessary in order to help remedy the problem of low home ownership rates in Latino communities. Whites who testified, on the other hand, tended to make general statements saying that discrimination is wrong and that the agency should do a better job. With the exception of the ranking minority member, nonminority Democrats tended to participate less in this hearing.

Minority legislators of the 107th Congress were also active in sending clear directives to federal agencies to engage in activities that benefit minority constituents. For example, in an oversight hearing relating to racial profiling, Congressman William Lacy Clay (D-MO) asked the DOJ to take a larger role in helping to enforce anti-discrimination laws: "Here's what I'm interested in: in seeing the DOJ come up with a concerted effort, a coordinated strategy to address those areas that we know are problems. And in the Missouri study, for example, we found that there were pockets and areas where police departments had very high incidents of stops and searches" (*The Benefits of Audio-Visual Technology in Addressing Racial Profiling*, 57)

The interventions for stronger enforcement by federal agencies clearly have a partisan slant as well. Most Democrats who participated in the oversight hearing indicated a preference for stronger efforts by the agency, while Republicans usually defended the status quo or did not want an increased effort by the agency, arguing that HUD was doing a good job enforcing existing fair housing laws without further funding or new legislation.

As shown in figure 4.3, black legislators spent the most time supporting minority-interest policies in the 107th Congress, as measured by their predicted level of support of 49 lines. Latino legislators were the next highest at 19 lines. Whites who took the pro–civil rights position did not spend equivalent time pressing federal agencies to be more vigorous in their enforcement actions, with a predicted rate of 3 lines. When examining all legislators who intervened in hearings—committee members and noncommittee members—Latino legislators begin catch up to black legislators. Latino legislators' line count rises to 31 lines, compared to 37 lines for black legislators and only 3 for white legislators (see figure 4.4). When committee leadership is factored in, the differences between black and white legislators were even greater, less so for Latinos. For example, black congressional leaders spent more time advocating for stronger enforcement than white leaders, with a predicted rate of 135 lines compared to 9 lines for whites.[3] Again, it is not that white legislators did not support civil

[3]There is only one Latino ranking minority member in the committee sample and the committee and noncommittee sample, and thus it is not possible to estimate its effect in a multivariate model.

rights, but simply that they did not engage in deliberations to the same extent as minorities. Indeed, there are some individuals who are vocal, such as Barney Frank, but the average white legislator does not exhibit this level of commitment.

Similar patterns persist when examining interventions by members of the Democratic Party, which is the party of almost all Latino and black legislators. Again, black and Latino legislators, whether these are just committee members who intervened or all legislators who intervened, outpace white legislators in the amount of time they spend advocating for minority interests. Figure 4.5 demonstrates that black Democrats in the committee sample contributed 57 lines, compared to 36 lines for Latino Democrats and 6 lines for white Democrats. When all participants, committee members and noncommittee members, are examined, as shown in figure 4.6, Latino Democrats move ahead of blacks in advocacy, at 70 lines compared to 49 for blacks and 8 for white Democrats. Representative Joe Baca's intervention in USDA discrimination against minority farmers plays an important role in explaining why Latino legislators devote more time to civil rights than blacks.

Beyond the Deliberations

Legislators influence the legislative agenda by pressing committee chairmen to hold oversight hearings. For example, Rep. Elijah Cummings (D-MD) was responsible for requesting a hearing on racial profiling (*The Benefits of Audio-Visual Technology in Addressing Racial Profiling*, 12–13). In addition to requesting the hearing, Representative Cummings was a major participant and urged the committee to enact legislation that would help correct the problem; he introduced a racial profiling bill for this purpose. Cummings also alluded to a CBC hearing to be held on the matter. In this instance, as in others, the CBC, by providing a forum for the collective discussion among legislators of a problem affecting black Americans, served to help reinforce the idea that black representatives should engage in collective action to solve the problems of a national constituency.

Congresspersons Eva Clayton (D-NC) and John Conyers (D-MI) were responsible for brokering an oversight hearing into the discrimination complaints lodged against USDA employees regarding discrimination against black farmers in the federal loan program. Clayton was the ranking minority on the subcommittee that held the hearing. She testified: "This hearing was agreed to almost 1 year ago by Chairman Combest and Ranking Member Stenholm during the House consideration of the farm bill, the offer to arrange for the hearing was made by the full committee leadership in consideration for the withdrawal of an amendment offered by Repre-

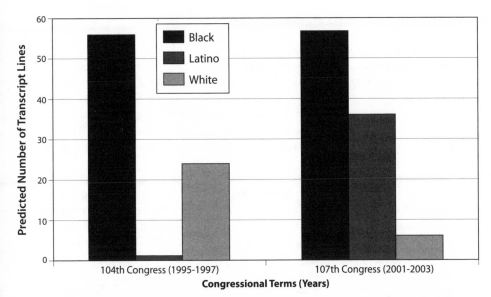

FIGURE 4.5 Intervention Levels by Committee Members for Stronger Civil Rights Enforcement by Race/Ethnicity, Democrats Only

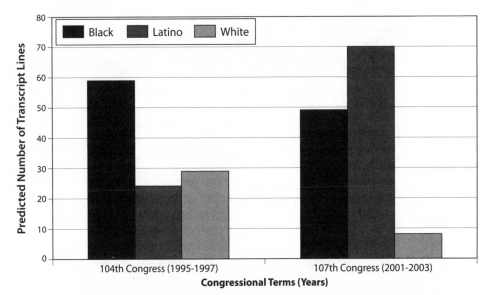

FIGURE 4.6 Intervention Levels by Committee and Noncommittee Members for Stronger Civil Rights Enforcement by Race/Ethnicity, Democrats Only

sentative John Conyers and myself regarding discrimination of services and programs by the Department of Agriculture. This hearing is a fulfillment of that agreement made earlier" (*U.S. Department of Agriculture's Civil Rights Program for Farm Program Participants*, 7). As this testimony indicates, brokering by key members of the Congressional Black Caucus made it possible for there to be a hearing on the plight of black farmers. In addition to brokering a deal with the subcommittee to drop a provision from the farm bill in exchange for the hearing, Clayton and Conyers were responsible for inserting a provision that created a director of civil rights at the USDA.

Walton (1988) argues that civil rights oversight hearings such as those described above have had "very little impact" on civil rights agency enforcement efforts (156). While actions by individual members of Congress may sometimes affect agency outputs, at other times they do not. The point of substantive representation is to devote time and effort to actively representing the point of view of your constituents in the legislative body (see Mill, *Considerations on Representative Government*).[4] When these efforts succeed, they can have an important impact. In the case of the USDA, for instance, Eva Clayton's interventions were responsible for getting the department to appoint a director of civil rights.

Conclusion

This chapter has shown that black legislators are statistically more likely than white legislators to intervene in agency policymaking for stronger enforcement of civil rights policies. In two of three Congresses examining racial issues, black legislators spent more time than white and Latino legislators in advocating for minority interests. Not only did black committee members engage in advocacy more than white committee members, but black legislators who were not members of committees engaged more than did whites who were not members. These findings provide support for the argument that strategic group uplift plays an important role in explaining the differences in advocacy of minority interests by white and racial and ethnic minority legislators in Congress.

The only time that black legislators were not more active than white and Latino legislators on racial issues was during the 103rd Congress, when

---

[4] I don't dismiss the likelihood of legislators to engage in substantive activity that will affect policies that affect their constituents, nor do I propose that symbolic representation is the only mechanism to which legislators should be held. However, engaging in this type of behavior is not cost free, and legislators could engage in other behaviors that could likely benefit their re-election efforts. Notwithstanding, I examine the substantive policy activity in which these legislators engage.

Bill Clinton was president. Since Clinton is a Democrat, as are most black legislators, it is not surprising that minorities' oversight activity was generally less aggressive in the first two years of his presidency. The 1995 Republican takeover of the House brought an increased level of oversight to combat Republican representatives' attacks on affirmative actions and other civil rights policies. Many black Democrats, such as Julian Dixon (D-CA) and Shelia Jackson-Lee (D-TX), played a vigorous role in defending the administration and ensuring that minority interests would be protected.

This chapter has also shown that Latino committee leaders, similar to black legislators, are more likely than white committee leaders to intervene in agency policymaking on civil rights. Latino committee leaders such as Nydia Velazquez (D-NY) and Matthew Martínez (D-CA) provided a voice for the interests of Latino and black constituents in advocacy for affirmative action programs and maintaining bilingual voting rights provisions. In doing so, they pursued strategic group uplift by mobilizing their resources as committee leaders.

While this chapter offers insight into the effect of race or ethnicity on legislators' behavior in explicitly racial/ethnic hearings, the next chapter tests the effect of race/ethnicity on legislative intervention in broader social welfare policy issues.

5

Congressional Oversight and Social Welfare Policy

IN THE 1992 presidential campaign, Democratic candidate Bill Clinton claimed that if elected, he would drastically reform welfare. True to his campaign promise, President Clinton supported a number of welfare proposals that included work requirements, time limits, and a reduction in benefits to legal immigrants. Many civil rights groups, to which a number of black and Latino members of Congress belonged, opposed these proposals because they believed they did not address the structural inequalities, such as lack of employment opportunities and racism in the labor markets that contributed significantly to welfare dependency. Minority legislators were also disappointed that a Democratic president would be espousing proposals based in negative stereotypes about welfare recipients—proposals of the sort usually advocated by conservative groups and Republicans. Although many welfare reform hearings were held on the various plans developed between 1993 and 1994, none of these proposals became law. Black and Latino legislators, serving as committee chairs in a House controlled by the Democratic Party, played an instrumental role in ensuring that these measures did not make it out of committee. After regaining control of Congress as a result of the 1994 election, Republicans renewed the call to reform welfare and pushed for more punitive measures of the sort opposed by Democrats. The end result was the passage of the Personal Accountability Act of 1996 by a Republican-controlled Congress, signed into law by President Clinton.

While the welfare reform debates of the early and mid-1990s received much public attention, they were not the only steps Congress took to help the poor during this period. Other policies, such as expanding health care coverage and increasing funding for affordable housing and community development, also drew substantial congressional attention. When Democrats controlled Congress, they worked to expand coverage of welfare programs such as Medicaid and food stamps, as well as to provide more funding for public housing. Conversely, Republicans were intent on cutting spending on these programs and giving state governments more control over welfare spending.

Social welfare policies of the sort discussed above have broad constituencies, but they disproportionately affect racial and ethnic minorities, who are more likely than white Americans to be poor. In this chapter, I examine the advocacy efforts of members of Congress for policies designed to help poor people as a second measure of the substantive representation of minority interests. I investigate whether the differences that exist between black, Latino, and white legislators in racial and ethnic hearings also occur in social welfare hearings. As in the previous chapter, I examine legislators' interventions in committee deliberations during part of the Clinton era (1993–1997) and the first term of the George W. Bush presidency (2001–2003). I focus on how actively legislators engaged in the deliberations in terms of questioning witnesses and interacting with fellow members of Congress. I also examine other legislative interventions, such as testifying at hearings in favor of social welfare policies that benefit the poor and requesting hearings designed to help poor people, who are disproportionately minorities. First, however, I provide an overview in the next section of how racial and ethnic diversity affected the composition of the various congressional committees that oversaw congressional discussions of social welfare policy in the following years, 1993–1996 and 2001–2003.

Racial and Ethnic Diversity of Congressional Overseers

The increase in the number of black and Latino members elected to Congress has diversified the congressional committees with responsibility for overseeing social welfare issues. Beyond the importance that blacks and Latinos place on civil rights and other racial policies, earlier studies have demonstrated that blacks and Latinos also have strong preferences for policies aimed at improving the socioeconomic status of racial and ethnic minorities. They tend to have more liberal preferences than whites when it comes to broader social welfare issues (Kinder and Sanders 1996; Leal 2007; Tate 1993). Thus, one can reasonably expect that legislators from districts that have a large number of black and Latino constituents are more likely to be represented on committees that have jurisdiction over social welfare programs such as Medicaid and welfare, because blacks and Latinos, who are disproportionately poor, often benefit from these programs.

Table 5.1 shows the racial and ethnic composition of the social welfare committee sample compared to the composition of the full House in the 103rd (1993–1995), 104th (1995–1997), and 107th (2001–2003) Congresses. Black legislators were slightly overrepresented on these committees: they comprised 14 percent in the 103rd Congress and 11 percent in the 104th and 107th Congresses, as compared to only 9 percent of the House in all three Congresses. In fact, the differences between black legislators on the committees are only statistically significant in the 103rd Congress, and not in the other Congresses. Latino legislators, by contrast, were overrepresented only in the 103rd Congress, when Democrats controlled

TABLE 5.1
Racial and Ethnic Composition of Committee Sample versus the Full House[*]

	103rd Congress (1993–1995)	104th Congress (1995–1997)	107th Congress (2001–2003)	Full House[*]
White	78%	87%	86%	87%
Black	14%	11%	11%	9%
Latino	6%	2%	2%	4%

[*]Full House composition is the same for each congressional term.

the assembly and the presidency, at 6 percent of committee members versus 4 percent in the full House. In both the Republican-controlled 104th and 107th Congresses, Latinos made up only 2 percent of the committee sample, versus 4 percent of the full House. The reduction in the percentage of black and Latino committee members in the Republican-controlled Congresses may have been due to the Republican leadership's decision to reduce the number of committees on which legislators could serve. In the previous congress, the rules regarding committee assignments were more flexible and allowed black and Latino legislators to serve on multiple committees that addressed issues relevant to minorities. Once the GOP changed the rules, however, minority legislators' ability to provide coverage on committees decreased (Canon 1999).

Additionally, because the residents of districts represented by blacks and Latinos tend to be disproportionately poor, one would expect to find a larger number of legislators on these committees from districts that have lower median family incomes than the full House average. Thus, when examining the likelihood that legislators will intervene in favor of implementing class-based policies, the deck may be implicitly stacked in favor of uncovering class-based differences. As expected, table 5.2 shows that in

TABLE 5.2
District Median Family Income of Committee Sample versus the Full House

	107th Congress (2001–2003) Full House (n = 435)	107th Congress (2001–2003) Committee Sample (n = 264)
Black	41,489	40,185
White and others	49,859	53,160
Latino	43,576	36,451

TABLE 5.3
Committee Members' Ideology Scores versus Full House Ideology Scores*

	103rd Congress Committee	103rd Congress Full House	104th Congress Committee	104th Congress Full House	107th Congress Committee	107th Congress Full House
Black	−.48	−.55	−.48	−.50	−.54	−.51
Latino	−.35	−.31	−.35	−.26	−.51	−.27
White	−.02	.01	.12	.12	.11	.13

*Source: DW-NOMINATE First Dimension Scores: http://www.voteview.com

the 107th Congress (2001–2003), black and Latino legislators represented districts with lower median family incomes than white legislators. Moreover, the median family income in the districts of the black and Latino legislators who served on the committees was lower than full House average of black and Latino legislators.

The evidence relating to whether legislators who served on these committees were more likely to have liberal preferences regarding social and economic policies than the full House was mixed but generally confirmed the expectation that committee members were more liberal. Again, I use the first dimension of the Poole and Rosenthal DW-NOMINATE score to assess each member's ideological disposition. This score reflects each legislator's roll-call voting behavior on economic and social policies. The score is on a scale from 1 to −1, where a 1 is conservative and a −1 is liberal. As shown in table 5.3, Latino committee members were more liberal than the House average for other Latino legislators in all three Congresses sampled. In two of the three Congresses, the white legislators on these committees were more liberal than fellow white legislators in the full House. However, only in the 107th Congress (2001–2003) were black committee members more liberal than the full House average for other black legislators. But even liberal white committee members were less liberal than the black legislators on the committees, who were no more liberal than black in the full House. The committees contained well-known liberal black legislators, such as John Conyers (D-MI) and Charles Rangel (D-NY); liberal Latino legislators, such as Henry B. González (D-TX) and Luis Gutiérrez (D-IL); and liberal white legislators, such as Barney Frank (D-MA) and Henry Waxman (D-CA). Considering that such liberal committee members will share similar policy preferences, the likelihood of finding racial or ethnic differences among legislators in terms of their level of advocacy for minority-friendly social welfare policy is smaller than for racial or ethnic policy.

The next section examines what impact the increase in the number of blacks and Latinos in Congress has had on congressional attention to social welfare issues in oversight hearings.

Congressional Attention to Social Welfare Issues and Legislative Responsiveness

Despite the spike in public attention devoted to welfare reform during the early to mid-1990s and the increase in the number of black and Latinos in the House, the level of congressional attention to social welfare issues did not change significantly from earlier years. Figure 5.1 shows the number of hearings devoted to social welfare issues such as Medicaid, welfare, and subsidized housing from 1991 through 2008. The percentage of hearings devoted to social welfare correlates slightly with which party controlled the House and the presidency in any given period, with Congress holding slightly more hearings under Democratic control than Republican control. Although the level of attention devoted to social welfare issues is broadly the same under Democrat and Republican rule, the agenda-setting power of the majority party plays a significant role in shaping the debate, determining which social welfare proposals receive a hearing and which proposals make it out of committee. Agenda control is usually an underappreciated factor in assessments of the representation of minority interests in committee oversight activities. From 1993 through 1995, Congress held approximately twenty-one hearings on welfare reform, but not one bill made it to the floor for a roll-call vote. In 1995–1997, when Republicans controlled the House, Congress held about twenty-four hearings that resulted in the two roll-call votes. The major welfare proposals were passed by the House and eventually signed into law. Thus, examining roll-call votes as the only measure of substantive representation of minority interests conceals the level of intervention and activity by Democrats and minority legislators to keep punitive welfare reform proposals from passing and to push for more liberal antipoverty programs.

In addition to the difference in agenda control, the tenor of the debate in the House was sharply different during the eras of Democratic and Republican control. The House held thirty-five hearings on Medicaid in the 103rd Congress (1993–1995) compared to twenty-eight held in the 104th Congress (1995–1997), but the focus in the 103rd Congress centered on expanding eligibility to the poor, while in the 104th Congress the debate focused on giving more power to the states. Instead of hearings directed to assisting the Clinton administration in achieving its policy objective to increase aid to the poor, the hearings were devoted to questioning the Clinton administration and agency officials relating to their efforts.

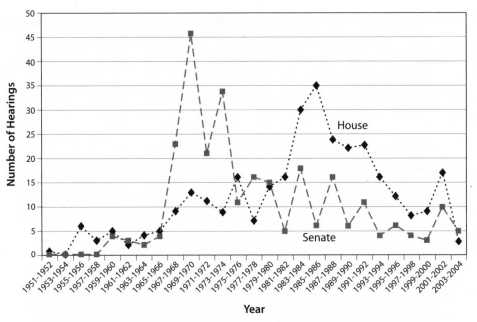

FIGURE 5.1 Congressional Attention to Social Welfare Issues, 1951–2004

The infusion of black and Latino legislators into the House may not have influenced the number of hearings devoted to social welfare, but it may have affected how much attention individual legislators paid to social welfare issues. In this context, did black and Latino legislators intervene at higher rates than white legislators? As with racial and ethnic oversight hearings, I examine the frequency with which members of Congress made verbal comments and submitted written statements to the record advocating for social welfare policies. Specifically, I considered this activity contained within transcripts of legislative oversight hearings from the US House of Representatives, 103rd (1993–1995), 104th (1995–1997) and 107th Congresses (2001–2003). For each Congress, a broad sample of hearings relating to social welfare policies were coded (see discussion in chapter 4 and appendixes B and C for details). The hearings represent a mix of issues ranging from affordable housing to health care. The committees represent a cross-section of types, from constituency-based to prestige committees.

In the 1990s, civil rights groups such as the NAACP supported racial/ethnic redistricting in efforts to get more blacks and Latinos elected to Congress. They believed that black and Latino legislators would be more supportive of a social welfare policy agenda than white liberal legislators. Although white liberals were more inclined to support class-based policies than policies with a racial specific focus, the leadership of civil rights groups believed that white legislators would not address the specific disparities in social welfare policies that resulted from racial and ethnic inequalities. The rest of the chapter investigates whether black and Latino legislators in fact proved to be more responsive to the social welfare interests of minorities than white legislators in committee oversight deliberations.

Liberal Social Welfare Policy and the Clinton Years

Although black and Latino legislators were part of the new Democratic majority following Clinton's election to the presidency in 1992, many civil rights and social welfare advocates were fearful that Clinton would reduce funding for social programs that benefitted the poor. These fears were not without merit, because Clinton had run as a "New Democrat" and promised to "end welfare as we know it" through significant reform of the welfare system. In 1993 President Clinton supported the Work and Responsibility Act. Health and Human Services officials spent much time testifying before House congressional committees regarding the Clinton administration's welfare policy. Clinton focused on personal accountability for adults but also advocated for child care and reforming the health care system. He wanted to place a two-year time limit on how long welfare recipients could receive benefits. Welfare recipients would be provided with job training in preparation for private- or public-sector jobs.

Most Democrats supported elements of the president's plan, but they were strongly against the time limits. The multivariate results, derived from the count model presented in table 5.4, show that in congressional committee hearings, black, Latino, and white legislators showed no significant difference in terms of the amount of time they spent advocating for minority interests.[1] The amount of time spent advocating for minority interests or interventions is measured by examining the number of transcript lines attributed to individual legislators who supported stronger implementation of general social welfare policy. White legislators spent just as much time in the deliberations arguing against the punitive measures of the Clinton proposal as black and Latino legislators did; it was party that determined the extent of legislators' interventions. This may indicate that black and Latino legislators are not as committed to advocacy for social welfare than they are to advocacy on racial or ethnic issues. Or the opposite could be true: black and Latino legislators' commitment may

---

[1]Since the variable of interest is how much legislators advocate for minority interests once they decide to intervene in oversight hearings, I only present the results of the second stage of the zero-inflated negative binomial count model. The results of the first stage of the model are presented in appendixes H–J.

TABLE 5.4

Interventions by Members of Congress for Stronger Implementation of General Social Welfare Policies in the 103rd Congress (1993–1995)

Explanatory Variables	Committee Members	Committee and Noncommittee Members
Party	.86**	.85**
	(.27)	(.24)
Black	−.87	−.86
	(.46)	(.41)
Latino	−.11	−.09
	(.58)	(.57)
Chair	.94**	.91**
	(.40)	(.37)
Black chair	.94**	.80*
	(.46)	(.45)
Ranking minority member	.36	.20
	(.33)	(.30)
% black voting-age population	.002	.004
	(.011)	(.009)
% Hispanic voting-age population	−.004	−.006
	(.006)	(.006)
Median family income	−.002	.01
	(.017)	(.02)
South	.03	.05
	(.29)	(.24)
Electoral safety	.02**	.03**
	(.01)	(.01)
Member of assigned committee	—	.12
		(.25)
Constant	2.22*	1.97*
	(.99)	(1.03)
Log pseudo-likelihood	−410.69	−467.53
Wald chi-square (11)	242.02	272.13
	(p<.001)	(p<.001)
Alpha	.39	.41
	(.22)	(.20)
N	201	216

Robust standard errors are in parentheses.
*Statistically significant at .05 level, one-tailed test.
**Statistically significant at .01 level, one-tailed test.
+Statistically significant at .10 level, one-tailed test.

be the same across the board, while white legislators may be more likely to intervene on social welfare issues. Indeed, the level of intervention by white legislators increased significantly in social welfare hearings compared to their intervention in the racial/ethnic hearings, particularly among white Democrats. The finding in table 5.4 confirms that Democrats, whether they served on the committee or not, were likely to devote more time to intervening in favor of minority interests than Republicans. Since the end of the civil rights movement, whites have been more willing to embrace class-based solutions to inequities than racial remedies (Hamilton and Hamilton 1997).

Personal experiences and the greater universality of social welfare issues may explain why there are not significant differences between rank-and-file minority members and white members on social welfare (Burden 2007; Fenno 2003). For example, Lynn Woolsey (D-CA), a white female legislator and former welfare recipient, advocated for increasing child support enforcement efforts to encourage fathers to pay. Woolsey attributed her understanding of the plight of single mothers who receive public assistance to her personal experience as a single mother on welfare (*Welfare Reform Proposals . . . Work and Responsibility Act*, 4): "I know firsthand the merits and faults of our welfare system, because in 1968 I was a divorced working mother, struggling to raise my three small children. The breakup of my marriage had left me without child support, without health care, and without child care for my children. And in order to survive, I turned to welfare to supplement my earnings. My experience, Mr. Chairman, on welfare and the knowledge that other families often need much more help than I did to get back on their feet, never leaves me" (535). Like many other Democrats, Woolsey did not support reducing benefits, but rather backed efforts to reduce the need for welfare assistance. She introduced legislation that emphasized stronger child support enforcement, affordable health care and child care, and jobs that pay livable wages. Her legislation would also have eliminated rules that keep two-parent families from receiving benefits.

Although the multivariate results in table 5.4 show no racial or ethnic differences between rank-and-file members, they also indicate that black committee leaders or chairpersons spent more time engaging in the deliberations in support of black and Latino interests than white committee leaders did. Generally, committee leaders have resources, such as additional staff, that allow them to be more active in committee activities than do rank-and-file members. Due to these resources, black committee leaders were more likely than black rank-and-file members and white committee leaders to engage in strategic group uplift through social welfare hearings. Figure 5.2 illustrates that black committee chairs devoted the most time to

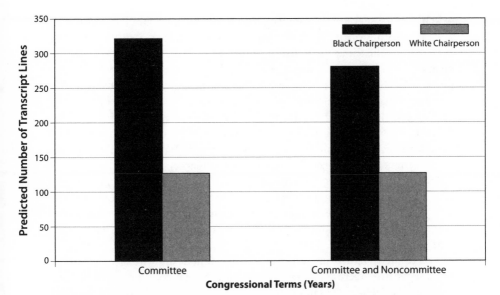

FIGURE 5.2 Intervention Levels by Committee Chairpersons for Stronger Implementation of General Social Welfare Policies by Race/Ethnicity in the 103rd Congress (1993–1995)

these hearings, at 320 lines compared to 124 for white committee chairs. When all participants at the committee level are taken into account, black committee chairs still intervened at a higher rate, with 280 lines compared to 124 for whites. These legislators advocated in the 103rd Congress by fighting for primary health care services for the underserved, affordable housing, welfare reform, and poverty reduction. Because Democrats controlled the House, black Democrats played an instrumental role in determining which proposals received a hearing and in shaping the overall debate. Black committee leaders were able to put their imprint on the legislation that came through committee. For example, Rep. Harold Ford Sr. (D-TN) was the chair of the House Ways and Means subcommittee. Ford's committee conducted many of the hearings on welfare reform proposals. Ford, whose district is majority black and contains the city of Memphis, spends a significant portion of his time advocating for minority interests. Although Ford is liberal, his moderation is reflected in his level of advocacy for welfare reform. Like most black and Latino legislators, Ford believes that structural problems such as high unemployment and high poverty rates are the primary reasons for high crime and lack of family stability, but unlike many Democrats, he supported some level of devolution of power to the states in determining welfare eligibility and benefits.

While Ford served as a gatekeeper in preventing welfare legislation un-favorable to minorities from passing out of committee, Rep. Floyd Flake (D-NY) did the same for housing policy. Rep. Flake was a subcommittee chair of the Housing Committee for the House Financial Services Com-mittee. As chair, he spent significant time arguing that HUD should do more to make it possible for low-income families to get loans in order to buy affordable housing: "It has always been my sincere belief that our Na-tion's existing financial infrastructure has the capacity to revitalize all of America's distressed communities," he reported. "What is needed now is a willingness to recognize this vast potential market and incentives to en-courage all financial service entities to participate in this rebuilding pro-cess. Indeed I often suggest that one of the most fertile fields of opportu-nity that has often been ignored by financial entities has been these communities that are underserved" (*HUD's Report to Congress on the Fed-eral Home Loan System*, 1).

The unified Democratic control of government and the fact that many black legislators were heading the committees that took up social welfare issues are key elements in understanding how strategic group uplift worked in social welfare hearings in the 103rd Congress. Black rank-and-file legis-lators "strategically" decided to defer to black committee chairs because they knew that the committee chairs would protect the interests of their black constituents. When the political context later changed and Demo-crats lost their majority, they also lost their ability to control the social welfare agenda, as demonstrated later in this chapter; and in this situation all minority legislators, regardless of whether they held a leadership posi-tion, had to directly engage in more advocacy for minority interests. La-tino legislators were not able to defer to Latino committee leadership to the same extent, because they represented less than 0.1 percent of the committee leadership positions, compared to 2 percent for blacks and 98 percent for whites. The only Latino committee leader in the sample was Rep. Henry B. González (D-TX), and thus it was not possible to estimate the impact of Hispanic leadership in the multivariate analysis.

Diversity of Perspectives and Challenging Negative Stereotypes in Social Welfare Debates

Examining the substance of legislators' comments and actions can be just as important as gauging how much time they spend engaging in commit-tee deliberations (Mansbridge 1999; Williams 1998; Young 2000). Although the multivariate results show that white legislators were just as active as black and Latino legislators in advocating for the interests of poor people in the 103rd Congress, a closer analysis of the deliberations reveals qualitative differences between black and white members relating to the specific issues they chose to highlight during the hearings. Black and Latino legislators spent more time than white legislators contesting negative stereotypes about the lack of work ethic among minority welfare recipients, instead framing welfare dependency as a problem caused mainly by structural inequalities in the job and housing markets that make it difficult for poor people to get off welfare. These legislators also contested existing negative stereotypes about welfare recipients. While many agreed with President Clinton and Republican legislators about the importance of personal accountability, minority legislators did not spend much time focusing on such issues as out-of-wedlock birth or weak parental responsibility as the main causes of welfare dependency.

In a hearing on a welfare proposal supported by President Clinton before the House Ways and Means's Subcommittee on Human Resources, black Congressman Donald Payne (D-NJ) argued that the vast majority of people who are on public assistance are impoverished and must be on welfare out of necessity and not by choice. He argued that many welfare recipients would work if jobs that paid livable wages were available and child care and housing were affordable. Payne further argued that the president's plan was too punitive: "Currently, the welfare system in this country is one that fosters cycles of dependency, an individual cannot get off welfare rolls because she cannot get a job that will provide a decent living wage for herself and her family, get quality child care, and get adequate housing at an affordable price. Providing jobs and job security will change this type of system to one that promotes and encourages self-sufficiency; however, we are unable or unwilling to invest the necessary resources in our families" (*Welfare Reform Proposals . . . Work and Responsibility Act*, 27). Payne's position is consistent with those of many black Democrats who have long argued that high unemployment is one of the leading causes of welfare dependency and only strong government intervention to create jobs will help break the cycle. In the 1970s and 1980s, in fact, black members of Congress introduced legislation calling for full employment.

Since job creation was the primary focus of most minority legislators, they argued that punitive measures focusing on individual-level behavior would do little to solve welfare dependency. Although President Clinton's plan provided job training and other efforts to increase the availability of jobs, black legislators argued that the plan did not go far enough in removing people from poverty. Here is Payne again:

> President Clinton's plan imposes a 30-month lifetime limit on AFDC benefits. However, without the adequate support systems in place—opportunity

for employment, day care, and an adequate salary to promote and encourage self-sufficiency—taking the punitive approach to dropping people from the welfare rolls may cause more harm than good. To his credit,
the President has proposed instituting a WORK "jobs" program into
the welfare system. However, this provision does not reach far enough
in lifting people out of poverty. WORK jobs will only allow an individual to earn the AFDC stipend plus $120 a month in work expenses.
Therefore, WORK is not designed to lift people out of poverty, it just
imposes another penalty for failure to "make do" with benefits that are
not adequate to raise, much less sustain, a family at poverty level [which
is less than $12,000 for a family of three]. (27)

Many black legislators, including Representative Payne, rejected President
Clinton's proposal and instead opted to support a more liberal version of
a welfare reform bill that removed time limits and work requirements.
Payne cosponsored a bill that he felt took "a significant step toward addressing the real problem with the welfare system, allowing people who
receive assistance to have jobs and gradually move from the welfare rolls to
self-sufficiency, without penalizing them for going to work" (27). Rep. Ed
Pastor (D-AZ) offered a harsh critique of the administration's proposal
and of how the time limits perpetuated "stereotypes of poor women on
welfare." Speaking in support of the bill that Payne cosponsored, Pastor
emphasized "that our goal is not to end welfare but to end poverty" (*Welfare Reform Proposals . . . Work and Responsibility Act*, p. 572).

The advocacy efforts that black and Latino legislators provide for minority interests during the welfare reform deliberations are significant, because they challenge the prevailing wisdom that black legislators fail to
provide a voice for their politically weakest black constituents (Cohen
1999; Hancock 2004; Strolovitch 2007). Ange Marie Hancock (2004)
argued, for example, that during the 1996 congressional welfare reform
deliberations, CBC members did little to provide a voice to the subgroup
in the African American constituency that was most affected by the reforms: poor African American women. She found that black legislators
failed to challenge the negative myth of the "welfare queen" because
members feared that attention to poor black welfare mothers would further marginalize the interests of the vast majority of African Americans
who did not receive welfare. Much of Hancock's analyses center on the
welfare reform debate in the 104th Congress (1995–1997), which Republicans controlled. The political context had much to do with how minority
legislators advocated for minority interests during the welfare reform debates. When Democrats controlled the congressional agenda, as they did
during the 103rd Congress (1993–1995), black and Latino legislators,
especially the committee chairs, were able to frame the debate and con-

duct hearings that focused largely on structural inequalities that contrib-uted to welfare dependency. When the GOP controlled Congress, on the other hand, most of the hearings focused on individual-level factors, such as work ethic and out-of-wedlock births. Thus, minority legislators spent most of their time trying to frame their defense of welfare in terms of pro-tecting the rights of the children, because their structural arguments were inadequate in face of the conservative tide that demanded welfare reform.

After many hearings from 1993 to 1995, none of the flurry of welfare bills made it to the House floor for a vote, demonstrating the importance of agenda control by the party (Cox and McCubbins 2005). Although President Clinton and many other legislators claimed they wanted to re-form the welfare system, Democrats could not agree upon the best way to do it. Thus, no significant changes were made to the welfare system in the first two years of Clinton's term. The president wanted time limits, but most Democrats—among them most black, white, Latino, and Asian legislators—did not support this provision and vehemently argued that programs designed to end poverty were the best way to reduce dependency on wel-fare. The context of the battle changed when Republicans won control of Congress after the 1994 midterm elections.

The Republicans' Contract with America and Retrenchment of Social Welfare Policies

In 1995 the Republicans controlled both the House and Senate. Intend-ing to implement their Contract with America, Republican legislators pushed through several proposals that mandated work requirements for welfare recipients, provided block grants to states to administer the bene-fits, and capped federal contributions. Similar provisions had been vigor-ously opposed by Democratic legislators when they were in the majority and controlled both chambers just two years earlier in the 103rd Con-gress. Agencies such as the Department of Housing and Urban Develop-ment (HUD) and Health and Human Services became responsible for implementing many of the provisions. The Republican efforts to reform welfare were part of the party's overall strategy to reduce the budget defi-cit by scaling back on many social programs. Republican leaders recom-mended cuts in a number of programs that benefited minorities and low-income individuals, such as vouchers for Section 8 housing, welfare, food stamps, and unemployment insurance. The hearings held on social welfare issues in these years reflected the Republican focus on a lack of personal accountability as the main reason for welfare dependency, as well as the Republican belief in the corruption of landlords who receive Section 8 housing vouchers. Black and Latino legislators, alongside other Democrats, vigorously fought back against the Republican assault on many social welfare policies, leading the fight against cuts in Medicaid and welfare.

Many House committees held hearings on various welfare reform proposals that were circulating through the chamber. In May 1996, the House Ways and Means Committee's Subcommittee on Human Resources held two days of hearings devoted specifically to evaluating the Clinton administration's proposal and the GOP proposal. Subcommittee chairman E. Clay Shaw (R-FL) expressed the Republican position on welfare reform: "Get welfare out of Washington and return it to the states. This is the final pillar of welfare reform. We should abolish the federal entitlement to welfare and return the program over to the states. The Washington lawyers and bureaucrats have not gotten it right yet. It is time to get them out of the way. Here, too, I hope the administration will come around" (*Welfare Reform*, 6).

The multivariate analysis in table 5.5 demonstrates that unlike in the 1993–1994 Congress under the Democratic Party, when black legislators deferred advocacy to black committee chairs, rank-and-file black legislators were just as likely to advocate for minority interests in the 104th Congress as were leaders. Divided government and Republican control of Congress spurred minority legislators into action. When Democrats were in control, black legislators did not necessarily need to intervene to a great extent, and they made the strategic decision to allow black committee leaders to articulate black interests. Once these black legislators lost their committee leadership positions, however, all members, regardless of whether they held leadership positions, had to engage in oversight actions to protect minority interests. Black committee members, such as Representatives Conyers and Rangel, spent the most time of any racial or ethnic group advocating for more liberal social welfare policies. Black legislators stressed the need for continued federal governmental involvement in setting standards and providing funding for welfare. They were the leading Democrats in the fight against granting more power to the states and imposing time limits on beneficiaries. They opposed granting more power to the states because they believed the states would not provide adequate services to the poor and minorities. As mentioned in chapter 3, the opposition of blacks to the devolution of power to states is rooted in the battle by states, especially southern states, to deny social welfare benefits to blacks. Thus, attempts by Republicans to give more power to states represented a threat to the collective interests of blacks.

Although welfare reform received much of the attention during congressional debates, the Republican efforts to reduce the federal budget deficit did not focus solely on welfare reform. While there was some bipartisan support for expanding programs such as Medicaid, the ideological polarization that was reflected in the electorate was apparent in House

TABLE 5.5
Interventions by Members of Congress for Stronger Implementation of General
Social Welfare Policies in the 104th Congress (1995–1997)

Explanatory Variables	Committee Members	Committee and Noncommittee Members
Party	.92**	.86**
	(.23)	(.21)
Black	.78**	.88**
	(.37)	(.34)
Latino	1.27	2.09**
	(1.56)	(.87)
Chair	1.00	1.01
	(.61)	(.61)
Ranking minority member	.35	.31
	(.28)	(.26)
% black voting-age population	−.01	−.01
	(.01)	(.01)
% Hispanic voting-age population	.01	.00
	(.02)	(.01)
Median family income	.02	.02
	(.01)	(.01)
South	.10	.09
	(.21)	(.20)
Electoral safety	.01	.01
	(.01)	(.01)
Member of assigned committee	—	.79**
		(.31)
Constant	2.23**	1.48**
	(.68)	(.67)
Log pseudo-likelihood	−519.88	−564.43
Wald chi-square (10)	604.91	142.20
	(p<.001)	(p<.001)
Alpha	.65	.63
	(.16)	(.15)
N	196	211

Robust standard errors are in parentheses.
*Statistically significant at .05 level, one-tailed test.
**Statistically significant at .01 level, one-tailed test.
+Statistically significant at .10 level, one-tailed test.

deliberations. Even moderate Republican legislators such as Constance Morella (R-MD) and Christopher Shays (R-CT) were expected to adhere to the GOP party line; each spent time questioning the role of the federal government in effectively addressing affordable housing. While they did not go as far as conservatives such as Joe Scarborough (R-FL) to advocate that HUD get out of the housing business, they did question federal involvement in the enterprise. Republican leaders targeted many affordable programs administered by HUD. The GOP cut HUD's budget during the appropriations process and limited the amount of money that could be used for Section 8 housing vouchers. A House Government Reform and Oversight subcommittee conducted a hearing that examined HUD programs and operations. HUD secretary Henry Cisneros testified before the committee regarding the efforts of his department to provide affordable housing to people. In this hearing, black Democrats praised the reorganization effort of Secretary Cisneros, while Republicans were wary of the administration's reform attempts. Minority legislators uniformly expressed the belief that the federal government and HUD should continue to play an important role in providing affordable housing for low-income individuals.

Civil rights groups such as the NAACP have long maintained that the federal government should take a strong role in providing social welfare services because of the history of states, especially southern states, discriminating against and refusing services to racial and ethnic minorities. Black legislators defend the necessity of keeping HUD or other agencies of the federal government involved in making sure that low-income individuals are provided with housing. Democrats such as Chaka Fattah and Ed Towns advocated for the poor in the 104th Congress by promoting the use of scattered site housing instead of high-rise public housing projects. They also fought for the Section 8 subsidy to be used by tenants to build equity in homes rather than being used by landlords to pay their mortgages.

Republicans, on the other hand, voiced skepticism regarding the federal government's role in protecting low-income housing. Conservative and moderate Republicans argued that state government and the private sector would be better suited to fulfill housing needs. Christopher Shays (R-CT), the chair of the subcommittee, made this point in his remarks: "There's no reason why we can't think of the States doing it. There's no reason why we can't think of other departments doing it. There's no reason why we can't think of the private sector doing more. There's really no reason why we can't go in any different direction, if that makes sense, based on what we think the mission is" (*Oversight Hearing on the Department of Housing and Urban Development*, 80).

Rep. Towns (D-NY) defended the administration's efforts by articulating the need for HUD to provide affordable housing and enforcement of fair housing laws. He stated that despite fiscal mismanagement associated with the agency, it was necessary for HUD to survive, as it performed an essential government function:

> I do not agree, however, with what may be the sentiment of some here today that we abandon ship and turn our backs on the millions of Americans who continue to rely on HUD's help. There exists no other Federal effort to undertake HUD's monumental mission. And if we abandon HUD, we just as surely abandon our major metropolitan areas and the people who live there. Shelter is a basic need, a human right and a national ideal. As we visit this issue, let us remember that as caretakers of the public good, our first commitment should be to that ideal: that every citizen deserves a place to call home. I welcome today's hearing as an important first opportunity to consider the administration's strategy for restructuring and revitalizing HUD. Mr. Secretary, I have reviewed the reinvention blueprint and await with interest your views on several aspects of this proposal. (4)

GOP member Joe Scarborough, in an exchange with Secretary Cisneros, advocated for the transfer of HUD's housing responsibilities to the states. He argued for the efficiency of this move (24). In response, Cisneros emphasized that the federal government has a vital role in facilitating housing programs, as the states do not have the capacity to do so. "My sense of it is that the Federal Government has been effective in the housing arena," he remarked. Noting that state agencies to provide housing finance were a relatively recent development and remained "very spotty, in terms of competence levels across the country," he urged that the assembly not "throw the baby out with the bath water" by transferring responsibilities from HUD to the states (24).

Cardiss Collins (D-IL), who was not on the committee, criticized what she perceived as waste and inefficiency in HUD but argued that the agency is necessary in providing affordable housing and community development: "For thirty years, the Department of Housing and Urban Development has served as the only Federal agency responsive to the housing, community development, and fair housing needs of millions of Americans. Yes, it has grown wasteful, overly bureaucratic, and in many ways, ineffective. But let's not pretend that because this agency and its mandate have become cumbersome it no longer has a vital role to play in this society" (4).

Figure 5.3 shows how much effort committee members devoted to articulating such positions in the committee hearings. The higher line counts indicate that legislators were spending significantly more time engaging the witnesses in the question-and-answer session and also in urging their colleagues not to enact punitive measures that would disproportionately affect the poor. Black committee members spent the most time advocating, with 51 lines compared to 14 lines for whites. The behavior of

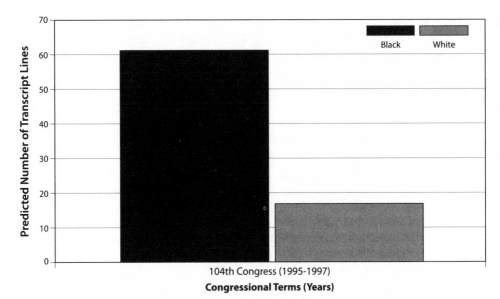

FIGURE 5.3 Intervention Levels by Committee Members for Stronger Implementation of General Social Welfare Policies by Race/Ethnicity

Latino committee members was not significantly different from that of white legislators.

In addition to examining intervention rates of legislators who are assigned to the committees responsible for conducting the hearing, it is important to examine the level of involvement in committee deliberations of legislators who are not assigned to relevant committees. Members who are not on committees intervened substantially in committee deliberations pertaining to issues such as the review of HUD's Section 8 multifamily housing and oversight of Medicaid. Black and Latino legislators were some of the staunchest defenders of these programs when they came under attack by Republican congressional leaders. They either attended or participated as invited guests of the congressional committee; some testified as witnesses in support of programs that would further the interests of minorities. Eva Clayton (D-NC), for example, testified at a subcommittee hearing that linked poverty to out-of-wedlock births. She provided a voice to describe the battle that young women face in trying to raise children with limited resources and the toll that poverty takes on their families.

In the end, minority legislators were not able to stop the Republicans from passing the measures they aimed to pass, nor could they prevent President Clinton, a fellow Democrat, from signing the welfare reform bill into law, but they mounted a vigorous defense of social welfare programs of particular interest to minorities, and they provided a voice to the voice-

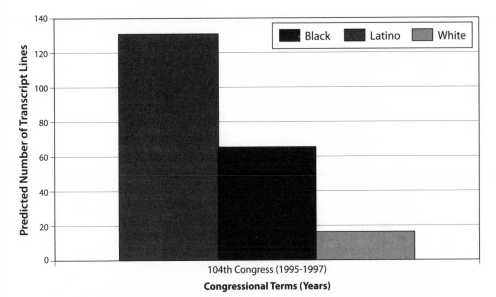

FIGURE 5.4 Intervention Levels by Committee and Noncommittee Members for Stronger Implementation of General Social Welfare Policies by Race/Ethnicity

less. Table 5.5 shows that when the interventions of all members who showed up at the hearings are taken into account, black legislators still intervened at higher rate than white legislators, but now Latino legislators were also more likely to advocate for minority legislators than white and black legislators. Figure 5.4 further illustrates the difference by showing how much time legislators spent advocating for Latino interests in social welfare hearings, with Latino legislators devoting approximately 131 lines compared to 65 for black legislators and 16 for white legislators.

Due to their smaller level of representation on these committees compared to black and white legislators, Latinos had to rely on all members in the CHC to provide effective advocacy for Latino interests. The impact of divided government, when different parties control the executive and legislative branches, on strategic group uplift provides insight into why Latinos intervened in the hearings much more in the 104th Congress (1995–1997) than the 103rd (1993–1995). In the 103rd Congress, Democrats controlled the House and did not attempt to reduce welfare benefits for legal immigrants. The Republican takeover of the House and their attempts to eliminate social welfare benefits for legal immigrants explains in part why Latino advocacy increased in the 104th Congress. Thus, legislators are very cognizant of where it makes the most sense to devote their resources in practicing strategic group uplift. This explains why Latino legislators, with their smaller numbers, chose to devote most of their advocacy to social welfare issues—given the looming threat of legal immigrants' losing their benefits—than to racial/ethnic issues during this period. Under unified Democratic control during the 103rd Congress, Latinos did not need to do this to the same extent.

Diversity of Perspectives in Deliberations

As demonstrated earlier for the period of Democratic rule of Congress and the presidency from 1993 to1995, considering the diverse perspectives that legislators bring to public policy decision making is just as important to the substantive representation of minority interests as measuring how much legislators intervene. In one of many congressional hearings relating to welfare reform, Dr. Mary Jo Bane, assistant secretary for children and families, US Department of Health and Human Services, testified before the Subcommittee on Human Resources on the Clinton administration's proposal. During her testimony, she emphasized that Clinton wanted to reform the welfare system and replace it with a system that "demands responsibility, strengthens families, protects children, and provides states with broad flexibility" (*Welfare Reform*, 8). The administration's position was echoed by committee Democrats, who called for welfare reform that emphasized personal responsibility and a commitment to work. Democrats, such as Rep. Barbara Kennelly of Connecticut, were against the granting of block grants to states without imposing sets of federal standards, fearing that such a process would result in "the poor, the elderly, the disabled, and children fighting for very, very limited resources" (*Welfare Reform*, 8). The Clinton welfare proposals required that people return to work within a two-year time frame, and after five years all cash benefits would end. Teenage mothers were required to live at home. Republicans opposed providing welfare benefits to recent immigrants. E. Clay Shaw, chairman of the committee, was generally opposed to providing welfare to noncitizens. "If you're not an American citizen, you should not automatically get welfare," he remarked. "To me, this is common sense. America is and will always be a land of opportunity for immigrants, but no one should come here looking for a handout." Shaw recommended "tougher standards so that welfare does not go to people who are not American citizens (6).

Even though black and Latino Democrats shared the general Democratic critique of the Republican proposal, they provided diverse perspectives in this critique. Their presence helped to counter the stereotypes that many conservatives referenced in discussing the causes of welfare dependency and who was most likely to benefit from social welfare programs. Although white Democrats advocated positions that closely aligned them with minority constituents, they revealed differences in perspective, and they highlighted different issues regarding racial or ethnic group interests. A leading advocate of providing benefits for legal immigrants, for example, was Rep. Xavier Becerra (D-CA). Whether by engaging in oversight activities on committees on which he served or attending meetings of committees that he was not on, Becerra argued that legal immigrants, as contributing members to society, should have the same access to social welfare benefits as citizens. For example, in his testimony before the House Ways and Means's Subcommittee on Human Resources, Becerra stated that "people who are lawful permanent residents in this country, having been granted permission to be here and have every right now to be here and ultimately will become US citizens." Becerra, noting that the Republican proposals seemed to achieve "most of their savings from eliminating access to services at the Federal level and at the State level to legal immigrants," highlighted the unfairness of this approach: "I have heard no one say these legal immigrants should stop paying the same State, Federal, local taxes, same property taxes, same business taxes, same sales taxes that we as citizens pay to have access to government services, but I do understand there is an effort now to ban their access to some of these programs." Although Becerra was in a district that was majority Hispanic and had a high proportion of legal immigrants, his perspective on whether social welfare benefits should be reduced for legal immigrants was influenced by his ethnic group attachments to Latinos and their immigrant experience. This attachment was greatly shaped in part by the experiences of his mother: "I was asked by my mother the other day how this would have affected her," he noted. "She has been a citizen for over 25 years. I had to tell my mother, had she come into this country after—she came in 1950 or 1952—had she come in under the circumstances that confront some of the folks that are coming legally into this country, she probably would not have access to certain services, although she has worked her entire life, never been on welfare" (*Welfare Reform*, 55–57).

In addition to being able to draw upon personal experiences that reinforce his group attachment, Becerra was a member of the Congressional Hispanic Caucus and faced pressure to represent all Latinos nationally. These factors combined highlight how strategic group uplift motivates Becerra to intervene in ways that will benefit his constituency of legal immigrants while at the same time allowing him to fulfill an obligation to uplift the interests of Latinos nationally. The Latino experience that undergirds strategic uplift is what makes his intervention in committee deliberations different from that of other Democrats.

At this same hearing, Becerra's fellow Democrat Charles Rangel (D-NY), who is black and represents a similarly constructed district that is 43 percent Latino and 5 percent black, with a high proportion of legal immigrants and a high poverty rate, provided a different perspective in his outspoken attempts to protect the rights of the poor and of minorities. During the two-day hearing, Rangel did not devote as much time to advocating to maintain welfare benefit eligibility for legal immigrants. The only time that he discussed this subject was during Becerra's testimony regarding how welfare reform would likely affect legal immigrants who were waiting to become citizens. When Rangel intervened, like most Democrats, he was supportive of Becerra's position and critical of GOP efforts to deny legal immigrants access to welfare benefits in order to cut government spending. "Rather than proposing a law that says if you are not a US citizen, you do not have access to anything, I think we can find something to receive equity and still tighten up and find savings someplace else," he remarked (*Welfare Reform*, 57). Although Rangel supported providing welfare benefits for legal immigrants, he did not articulate this support in terms of the personal experiences and concerns of legal immigrants in a similar manner to Becerra, nor was Rangel charged with representing the interests of Latinos nationally.

Meanwhile, Pete Stark (D-CA), a white legislator, again from a similarly constructed district, did not provide the same level of advocacy for legal immigrants. In fact, Stark was a member of the committee responsible for conducting the hearings, but he did not intervene in the hearing. Contrasting the remarks of these legislators suggests that although Democrats usually articulate the position that most minority groups favor, there are key differences in the perspectives that they bring to debates in support of the social welfare of minorities. In congressional deliberations, black and Latino Democrats often provide opinions that agree with those shared by Democrats generally, but they sometimes offer different reasons for their views.

Social Welfare Policy in the Post-9/11 Era

In 2000 Republicans regained control of the presidency and maintained control of the Congress. George W. Bush won a highly contested presidential election against Al Gore, and his first item was tax cuts. The Republican Congress, despite battling with Democratic President Bill Clinton, had been successful in reducing spending on many social programs and was now poised to act on President Bush's call for tax cuts. According to Democrats, tax cuts to reduce the budget deficit would mean further cuts in federal social spending. Even though liberal Democrats, including black and Latino legislators, disagreed with Clinton over the details of his preferred social policy, they favored his policies much more than those of conservative President Bush.

Unified Republican control of government affected how much time black and Latino legislators devoted to advocacy of minority interests in committees. The multivariate results in table 5.6 shows that there was no

TABLE 5.6
Interventions by Members of Congress for Stronger Implementation of General
Social Welfare Policies in the 107th Congress (2001–2003)

Explanatory Variables	Committee Members	Committee and Noncommittee Members
Party -	.71**	.47*
	(.30)	(.25)
Black	−.18	−.47
	(.49)	(.44)
Latino	−.06	−.43
	(.34)	(.40)
Chair	.38	.07
	(.39)	(.42)
Ranking minority member	.50	.51
	(.28)	(.30)
% black voting-age population	.01	−.51
	(.01)	(1.14)
% Hispanic voting-age population	.10	.05
	(.34)	(.61)
Median family income	.02	−.004
	(.01)	(.008)
South	−.17	−.17
	(.31)	(.27)
Electoral safety	.01+	.01+
	(.01)	(.01)
Member of assigned committee	—	−.47*
		(.26)
Constant	2.56**	3.51**
	(.86)	(.77)
Log pseudo-likelihood	−359.92	−444.90
Wald chi-square (10)	56.07	19.70
	(p<.001)	(p<.05)
Alpha	.41	.45
	(.20)	(.14)
N	264	283

Robust standard errors are in parentheses.
*Statistically significant at .05 level, one-tailed test.
**Statistically significant at .01 level, one-tailed test.
+Statistically significant at .10 level, one-tailed test.

significant difference in the amount of time minority legislators and white legislators spent in advocating for minority interests in the 107th Congress. Legislators, whether black, Latino, or white, spent roughly equal amounts of time at hearings directing comments at agency and local officials and calling for agencies to implement policies that extended coverage to less privileged socioeconomic groups. Black committee members devoted 11 lines to intervening for minority interests, compared to 6 lines for whites and 5 lines for Latinos. Comparing the intervention levels of committee and noncommittee members, black legislators spent 12 lines intervening, while white and Latino legislators spent 8 and 6 lines, respectively. These intervention levels are not statistically significant. The drop-off in intervention levels by all defenders of minority interests on social welfare policy was significant under Republican control of all branches of government compared to the 104th Congress (1995–1997), during which Democrats controlled the executive branch. Much of the activity in social welfare agenda in the 104th Congress revolved around GOP efforts to scale back social welfare benefits to minority constituents. President Clinton signed the welfare reform bill in 1996, and he was followed by a Republican president who supported the congressional Republicans' agenda to limit government and retrench on social welfare policies. In this context, congressional Republicans did not devote much attention to hearings on social welfare, limiting the opportunities that minority legislators had to intervene in on behalf of their constituents.

As expected, Democrats still intervened at higher rates in support of implementing more liberal social welfare policies favored by minorities. Committee Democrats spent an average of 19 lines intervening, compared to 2 lines for Republicans (see table 5.7). For example, in one oversight hearing pertaining to HUD's administration of the community development block grant program, Rep. Barney Frank (D-MA) stated that HUD officials should make a better effort to ensure that low- and moderate-income individuals were receiving most of the benefits of the program (*Review of Community Development Block Grant Program,* 2–3). Asian American representative Patsy Mink (D-HI), who was the ranking Democrat on the House Education and the Workforce Subcommittee on Twenty-First Century Competitiveness, proposed during a series of oversight hearings on the effects of welfare reform introducing legislation that would amend welfare reform to extend more benefits to low-income individuals:

> The past 5 years have been nothing less than disastrous for many welfare recipients. Most are still living below the poverty line; 30 percent have not found jobs. Those who have earn only around $7 an hour on average. With the median income among employed former recipients only

TABLE 5.7
Intervention Levels by Members of Congress for Stronger
Implementation of General Social Welfare Policies by Political
Party in the 107th Congress (2001–2003)

	Committee Members	Committee and Noncommittee Members
Democrats	19	20
Republicans	2	4

$10,924 in 1999, many families who have lost or left welfare cannot afford health insurance or child care and sometimes cannot pay for food or rent. . . . Later this month I will be introducing legislation that amends TANF in various ways. . . . TANF needs to be revised so that getting off welfare means being able to earn an education as well as enough money to support the family. (*Welfare Reform: An Examination of Effects*, 3–4)

The content of legislators' interventions into class-based policies was largely the same in the 107th Congress, but many minority legislators and legislators who had large minority voting-age populations in their districts did inject race into discussions of socioeconomic programs. For example, in an oversight hearing relating to extending Medicaid coverage to low- and moderate-income individuals before the House Energy and Commerce Committee's Subcommittee on Health, Congressman Gene Green, a white Democrat from a majority-Latino district in Texas, stated that the program should be expanded to address the health needs of Latinos. "While all Americans are struggling to find affordable health insurance," Green noted, "minorities are much more likely to be uninsured." He continued: "For example, Latinos comprise only 12 percent of the US population, but nearly one quarter of the uninsured. . . . I am a strong supporter of legislation such as the Family Care Act, sponsored by Ranking Member Dingell, which would expand Medicaid and S-CHIP coverage to low-income adults. I also support efforts to double the funding for our core safety-net providers, such as Community Health Centers, public hospitals, and state departments of health, and private hospitals" (*The Uninsured and Affordable Health Coverage*, 20–21).

Congressman Edolphus Towns, a black Democrat from a New York district that is 60 percent black and 16 percent Latino, made similar comments in this same hearing regarding expanding the program to meet the needs of Latinos: "Most uninsured Americans are minorities, low to moderate income level, adults between the ages of 18–24 and workers who are not offered or cannot afford insurance through the work place," he stated. Towns spotlighted Hispanics in particular as "the largest uninsured group" in the country. "Hopefully, today's hearings will begin to provoke the needed action in Congress to formulate legislation on this critical issue," he remarked (22).

The main difference between Democrats and Republicans in the sample is that Democrats made more specific statements calling for policy action by a given agency to either expand or implement existing programs to benefit minorities, while Republicans made general statements regarding agency efforts to implement programs to benefit low- to moderate-income individuals. Unlike in the racial or ethnic hearings discussed in chapter 4, however, more Republicans were willing to go on record to voice their opposition to the expansion of such programs. For example, in the hearings relating to extending Medicaid coverage to more lower-income groups, Rep. Ed Bryant (R-TN) opposed expanding the programs because of the costs: "Almost 1 in 4 in Tennessee, and so about 24-something percent of our folks, are on Tenn Care, and it is breaking our back financially. And I am not sure that we want a whole lot more dropped on us if you start talking about expanding the Medicaid, and things like that would impact us. And I am sure that other States are the same way. It is kind of an unfunded mandate to some extent, and we have to be careful as we look at going down those types of roads to get there" (9).

In addition to direct opposition to expansion, many Republicans supported the status quo in the administration of programs for the poor. Rep. Billy Tauzin (R-LA), for instance, minimized the problems of the uninsured and expressed support for President Bush's proposed solution to the undersupply of health care: "A strong and growing economy is the engine that allows us to make progress on social problems like access to affordable health care. Who are the uninsured? These are people generally above the official poverty level, and sometimes several times above that level. . . . The President has provided thoughtful leadership on this subject which deserves our support. He has proposed a refundable tax credit. . . . For lower-income Americans, the proposed health insurance credit generally covers more than half of the premium the purchaser would face" (24–25).

Black and Latino legislators, because they are overwhelmingly in the Democratic Party, have very little power to shape the agenda in a GOP-controlled Congress, nor do they have any sway over the Republican-controlled executive branch. As a result, minority legislators "strategically" devoted most of their efforts intervening mainly on racial/ethnic issues that threatened their constituents. Whites and minority legislators divided the responsibility to equally advocate for the interests of the poor. Thus, the party that controls government affects strategic group uplift. Whether government is divided or unified, minority legislators must decide on which issues they are going to spend their limited time and resources in advocating for minority interests.

Conclusion

The racial or ethnic background of legislators matters in terms of the level of their advocacy for minority interests and the interests of the poor. Although most Democrats spent time fighting various welfare reform proposals that would have imposed time limits for the receipt of benefits and introduced mandatory work requirements, black legislators consistently spent the most time engaging in these deliberations. Their advocacy encompassed everything from black committee leaders' decisions about which proposals would receive a hearing and the tenor of the debate in the Democratically controlled Congress in 1993–1994 to the appearance in 1995–1996 of black rank-and-file members at many welfare reform hearings to urge that welfare benefits for children should not be cut. During the welfare reform debates under GOP control, Latino legislators such as Xavier Becerra actively advocated for the poor and also against proposals designed to exclude legal immigrants from social services. In 1993, Latino legislators' level of intervention was not significantly different from that of white legislators; however, in 1995–1996, they intervened significantly more than did white legislators.

When Democrats controlled the House under Clinton, many rank-and-file black legislators deferred advocacy to subcommittee chairs. Although a number of bills to accomplish welfare reform were introduced and discussed in hearings, most of the proposals did not make it out of committee. When Republicans took control of the House, Democrats lost their committee leadership positions and were no longer able to control the agenda on social welfare issues. To honor the Contract with America, Republicans proposed deep cuts in social programs. Since blacks and Latinos are disproportionately poor and were major beneficiaries of these programs, black and Latino legislators fought vigorously against these reforms. Unlike in the 103rd Congress, black and Latino legislators' advocacy efforts were not able to stop the GOP from ending welfare as a federal entitlement program and imposing stricter time limits and work requirements. Congress also reduced funding for federal agencies, including the Department of Health and Human Services and the Department of Housing and Urban Development, charged with administering programs designed to help the poor.

When Republicans regained control of the presidency and maintained control of the House with the election of George W. Bush in 2000, Bush and GOP congressional leaders continued to focus on providing tax cuts and reducing the size of the federal budget. They once again targeted social welfare programs. The September 2001 terrorist attacks on the World Trade Center and Pentagon subsequently shifted congressional attention to national security issues. During this period, there was no significant difference between blacks, Latinos, and whites in terms of how much time they spent on social welfare advocacy.

In terms of the substance of interventions into social welfare policy, it is clear that black and Latino legislators improved deliberations relating to welfare reform by challenging many stereotypes about the root causes of welfare dependency. When Republicans argued that a lack of personal responsibility characterized welfare recipients, Democrats, and especially black and Latino legislators, countered that poverty was a structural problem that would require structural solutions. In hearings on welfare reform, legislators argued that welfare recipients wanted to work, but there were not sufficient jobs available that paid a living wage. Minority legislators also argued that adequate child care and educational opportunities were not available to break the conditions that cause dependency. Efforts by either the Democratic president or Republicans to base the welfare reform proposals on stereotypes were strongly rebuffed by black and Latino legislators.

6

Conclusion

IN MAY 2009 PRESIDENT BARACK OBAMA nominated US Court of Appeals judge Sonia Sotomayor to replace retiring US Supreme Court justice David Souter. If confirmed by the US Senate, Sotomayor would be the first Latino woman to serve on the nation's highest court. However, controversy ensued after the nomination over comments she made during a speech she delivered at various universities. In the speech, Sotomayor said, "I would hope that a wise Latina woman with the richness of her experiences would more often than not reach a better conclusion than a white male who hasn't lived that life."[1] Sotomayor's statement suggested that her sex and ethnicity would play a role in her evaluation of cases of sex and gender discrimination in ways unavailable to white judges. Some Republicans and conservative commentators strongly condemned this statement and questioned Sotomayor's ability to fairly decide cases that came before the Supreme Court. President Obama, as well as Sotomayor herself, started to distance themselves from these comments. The president said he was sure she would have restated her original comments. Sotomayor, in her Senate confirmation hearings, duly stated that she used a "poor choice" of words in making the "wise Latina" comment. Democrats believed these criticisms were unfair, because Supreme Court justice Samuel Alito during his confirmation hearings had referenced how his family's experiences of being discriminated against because of their Italian American background helped shape his outlook in evaluating discrimination cases. Sotomayor's liberal supporters believed that her background would be an asset in interpreting and applying the law in a just fashion, while her detractors believed that her background would make it difficult for her to objectively judge cases.

This scenario illuminates the larger question considered in this book regarding what role descriptive characteristics of public officials, such as race and ethnicity, play in influencing their decision making and to what extent race and ethnicity motivate their efforts in working on issues that come before Congress. Previous research finds that white Democrats are just as attentive to minority interests and sometimes provide better representation to minorities than black legislators (Swain 1993; Thernstrom 1987). The

[1]Savage, Charlie. "A Judge's View of Judging Is on the Record." *The New York Times*, May 15, 2009.

evidence from committee oversight hearings in the 103rd, 104th, and 107th Congresses suggests otherwise. Even though white members on these committees were just as liberal as black and Latino members, there were still substantial gaps in how much white and minority legislators advocated for the interests of minorities. Black and Latino legislators spent more time and effort advocating for the interests of minority consti-tuents on controversial issues such as racial profiling, employment discrimination, affordable housing, and welfare reform than did white legislators, and they also devoted significant time advocating for the social welfare of the poor.

In addition to examining how much effort legislators spend engaging in oversight, this account examined how legislators' racial or ethnic background informs committee deliberations among legislators and between legislators and federal officials on important public policies such as welfare reform and civil rights enforcement. Does the inclusion of more descriptive representation in deliberative bodies such as the US Congress improve public-policy decision making? Most advocates of racial and ethnic redistricting argue that descriptive representation contributes substantially to improve the substantive representation of minority interests. However, Lani Guinier (1995) argues that racial redistricting does not go far enough to provide minority substantive representation. She argues that the electoral rules and institutional rules of Congress need to be changed to give minority groups a chance to win office and bring about outcomes that favor them. The presence of black and Latino legislators alone is not sufficient to affect the outcomes if the rules remain unchanged. However, the presence of black and Latino legislators in Congress affects the deliberations and level of attention that is devoted to minority interests and other disadvantaged groups in oversight. I find that black and Latino legislators bring what Young (2000) refers to as situated knowledge and diversity of experiences to policy debates and affect the way issues are discussed in committees. For example, many scholars have argued that if women had been on the all-white male Senate panel that reviewed Anita Hill's sexual harassments claims against Clarence Thomas during the 1992 Senate confirmations, the proceedings would have more carefully considered Hill's claims of sexual harassment. I find that the presence of blacks and Latinos on congressional committees operates in a similar manner in terms of bringing minority perspectives to the decision-making process and informing the debate. These findings provide support for the value of descriptive representation.

I have argued that an ideology of strategic group uplift explains the differences between minority and white legislators. The concept of strategic group uplift suggests that racial and ethnic background—in addition to other factors, such as reelection motivations, party affiliation, constituent influence, and personal experiences—should be a central component of all congressional studies that evaluate what motivates legislators to engage in advocacy activities. Studying the impact of race and ethnic background on oversight also forces us to reevaluate what it means to substantively represent constituent interests by clearly establishing the link between committee deliberations and governing.

Implications for Racial, Ethnic, and Class-Based Politics

In *The Souls of Black Folk* (1903), W. E. B. Du Bois stated that the "problem of the twentieth century is the problem of the color-line." However, sociologist William Julius Wilson, in *The Declining Significance of Race*, argued that the life chances of blacks are being determined less by their racial background and more by their class. Thus, policymakers concerned with improving the status of blacks and other groups should focus on improving conditions that address class, because blacks are disproportionately poor and would benefit from these policies. The move from focusing on racial issues to nonracial issues is also reflected in the representational style of some politicians (Canon 1999). Legislators who came of age in the civil rights era, such as John Conyers and Charles Rangel, are slowly being replaced by new politicians, such as Barack Obama, Harold Ford Jr., Artur Davis, and Kendrick Meek. These newer black politicians, unlike the civil rights pioneers, tend not to highlight solutions to racial issues in their campaigns but instead to focus on issues that transcend race, such as class.

Despite the rise of a new generation of black and Latino politicians who tend to publicly distance themselves from talking explicitly about race in the US House of Representatives, the race and ethnicity of legislators continues to motivate their level of engagement on racial and ethnic, as well as broader class-based, issues. The findings in chapter 4 demonstrate that black and Latino legislators spend greater time and effort than their white peers advocating for the interests of blacks and Latinos in congressional hearings relating to racial and ethnic issues, such as enforcement of antidiscrimination laws in employment and housing. This increased advocacy is not just confined to members who are on the committees but also includes legislators who are not on the committees. The only time in the sample that black legislators were not more active than white and Latino legislators on racial issues was in the 103rd Congress (1993–1995), when Democrats controlled the House and Democrat Bill Clinton was president. Many black and Latino legislators joined forces in defending efforts to maintain affirmative action and bilingual voting rights provisions.

Both black and Latino legislators fight for minority issues for reasons to an extent that cannot be explained simply by their membership in the

Democratic Party and their having liberal ideological preferences. Many of the white Democrats who served on the committees in the samples analyzed in chapters 4 and 5 were significantly more liberal than other white legislators in the full House, yet there were significant ideological differences between them and black legislators. The ideological differences between white and Latino Democratic legislators on the committees were less dramatic but still significant. Strategic group uplift helps to explain the disparity in the different groups' advocacy for black and Latino interests: black and Latino legislators are products of communities that are more liberal on racial issues, and minority legislators are expected to act on their communities' views once they are in positions of power. The concept of strategic group uplift captures the interaction between legislators' desire to be reelected and their wish to fulfill the expectations of the African American and Latino communities by working to improve the socio-economic conditions of all blacks and Latinos nationally and internationally.

Black and Latino legislators not only devote significant time to advocating for pro-minority positions on racial or ethnic issues, they also exert a significant amount of effort working on social welfare issues. The fact that black and Latino legislators intervene at the same rate as white legislators to protect the social welfare interests of minorities—and even more often than white legislators during contentious welfare reform debate—counters concerns by critics that black and Latino legislators in majority-black and majority-Latino districts pursue only racial or ethnic policies that benefit their black and Latino constituents. The findings in chapters 4 and 5 show that black and Latino legislators pursue a "dual agenda" wherein they concentrate on eliminating racial and ethnic disparities while at the same time focusing on class-based policies that address the poverty that affects blacks, Latinos, and whites.[2] Various attempts by the Clinton administration and later the GOP-controlled House to limit welfare benefits were met with fierce resistant from Democrats, particularly black and Latino members. During the welfare reform debates, black and Latino legislators actively advocated for the poor and also against proposals designed to exclude legal immigrants from social services.

When Democrats controlled the House, black and Latino legislators relied upon black subcommittee leaders to keep welfare reform proposals from passing out of committee that would have hurt the poor and disproportionately affected racial and ethnic minorities. When Republicans took control of the House in 1995, minorities lost the power to control the

---

[2]Hamilton and Hamilton (1999) introduces the concept of the "dual agenda" when describing the strategy that civil rights groups used in fighting for both civil and economic rights.

agenda that they had under Democratic control. Still, black and Latino legislators fought vigorously against GOP efforts to cut social programs such as welfare, Medicaid, and affordable housing. Unlike in the 103rd Congress, black and Latino rank-and-file members were more active than their white counterparts. In the 103rd Congress, black and Latino committee chairs led efforts to stop the retrenching of social welfare benefits, but in the 104th Congress there was no difference between leaders and rank-and-file members. In the end, black and Latino legislators were not able to stop the GOP from reducing federal spending on social welfare programs. Agencies responsible for administering social welfare programs, such as the Department of Health and Human Services and the Department of Housing and Urban Development, saw their funding reduced by Congress. Also, Congress imposed stricter time limits and work requirements on welfare benefits and ended welfare as a federal entitlement program. In 2001, when Republicans controlled both the presidency and the Congress, black and white legislators still advocated at the same rate for social welfare issues. Black, Latino, and white legislators worked to ensure that Republican tax cut proposals and budget cuts would not unfairly impact the poor and minorities.

Implications for Coalition Politics

During the 2008 Democratic presidential primary between Senator Barack Obama (D-IL) and Senator Hillary Clinton (D-NY), many commentators questioned whether Latino voters would support an African American candidate for president. In states with large Latino populations such as California, Nevada, and Texas, Clinton overwhelmingly won the Latino vote over Obama. The disparity in the Latino support for Clinton over Obama prompted one political consultant to state that Latino voters would not support Barack Obama because he was black. Political scientists have found that tension persists between blacks and Latinos in competition for employment and housing opportunities (McClain and Karnig 1990; McClain 1993). This study demonstrates that while the tension that may exist among blacks and Latinos in the general public, it does not prevent black and Latino legislators from working together to support and defend both the black and Latino communities. Legislators such as Bobby Scott (D-VA) and Nydia Velazquez (D-NY) spent time advocating efforts to eliminate bilingual voting requirements, while Eva Clayton (D-NC) and Joe Baca (D-CA) worked together to ensure that the USDA eliminated obstacles in the farm lending program that discriminated against black and Latino farmers.

Implications for Political Representation

Many studies of political representation have been less than willing to recognize deliberations in Congress as a substantive activity when evaluating
the representation of constituent interests. Whether it is making a speech
on the floor or in committee, this behavior is typically treated as no more
than a symbolic act that contributes very little to substantive legislative
duties (Pitkin 1967). As a result, most of the studies on representation
focus mainly on the extent to which legislators' roll-call votes are consistent with minority groups' subjective or objective preferences on issues
(see, for example, Cameron, Epstein, and O'Halloran 1996; Hero and
Tolbert 1995; Lublin 1997; Miller and Stokes 1963; Swain 1993; Welch
and Hibbing 1984; Whitby 1997). This study joins a new and growing
literature that demonstrates the importance of expanding our idea of what
constitutes substantive representation beyond roll-call voting by examining how descriptive representation functions in another area of substantive
importance (Bratton and Haynie 1999; Canon 1999; Casellas 2009;
Gamble 2007; Grose 2003; Hall 1996; Haynie 2001; Minta 2009; Sinclair-
Chapman 2003; Tate 2003).

Normative political theorists argue that descriptive representation contributes substantially to deliberative democracy by providing distinctive
viewpoints to the policy-making process (Mansbridge 1999; Williams 1998;
Young 2000). The findings in chapters 4 and 5 provide firm support for
the important link between deliberations and governance and the value of
descriptive representation in this important function of Congress. No
matter what the issue dimension or the political party that controls the
Congress or presidency, black and Latino legislators consistently provided
alternative viewpoints and policy prescriptions in oversight of such key
policy issues as welfare reform, affordable housing, and civil rights enforcement. For example, while most Democrats are generally against efforts by Republicans to make English the official language of the United
States and to reduce funding for bilingual education programs, there are
clear distinctions in how white and minority legislators respond to these
efforts. Latino legislators usually bring to bear their experiences of being
discriminated against and how these proposals impact the Latino community more broadly.

Black and Latino legislators also tend to draw on their experiences as
part of marginalized groups to direct attention to issues that white legislators neglect. They influence the Democratic Party to pay more attention
to these issues by requesting hearings and agreeing to testify at the hearings. Reps. Eva Clayton (D-NC) and John Conyers (D-MI), for instance,
requested that hearings be held on the plight of black farmers. Rep. Mat-

thew Martínez (D-CA) requested that hearings be held on affirmative action in employment. Rep. William Clay Sr. (D-MO) argued that affirmative action did not benefit unqualified racial or ethnic minority job applicants but rather that qualified minorities who do not otherwise have opportunities because of racial or ethnic discrimination.

Black and Latino legislators can and do serve as a powerful voice for groups that have been marginalized, and their presence in hearings can greatly shape the nature of the debate. Minority legislators challenge and dispel negative stereotypes about blacks and Latinos that arise in policy debates. Some scholars who study the intersection of race, class, and gender have questioned if descriptive representatives can provide a voice to all members of the group they represent (Cohen 1999; Hancock 2004; Strolovitch 2007; Young 2007). Most of this literature has centered on black legislators and the claims by the CBC to represent the interests of all blacks. Such studies argue that legislators do little to advocate for the interests of black gays and lesbians on HIV/AIDS policy or for poor black welfare mothers. According to Hancock (2004), when black legislators had an opportunity to defend welfare mothers, they did not do so. My study shows, by contrast, that black legislators as well as Latino legislators play a vital role in advocating for all blacks and Latinos in the public policy-making process. This role was evident during the welfare reform debates in the mid-1990s. While Republicans advanced arguments based on stereotypes about welfare recipients' personal behavior, black and Latino legislators denounced their negative characterizations of welfare recipients. For example, Rep. Ed Pastor (D-AZ) passionately defended poor black and Latino women against commonly held perceptions that they are lazy and not willing to work. He stated that welfare dependency by poor black and Latino women is not caused by a lack of desire to work but by their inability to find affordable child care and jobs that pay living wages. Pastor was even critical of some provisions in the Clinton administration welfare reform proposal, which, he argued, were based on negative stereotypes about poor women on welfare.

Legislative Responsiveness and Democratic Accountability

Critics of racial and ethnic redistricting argue that majority-black and -Latino districts are safe districts, and the legislators who serve in them will be less responsive to the needs of black constituents, since it is through elections that citizens hold government and its representatives accountable (Swain 1993). I show, however, that black and Latino legislators—many of them from safe districts due to redistricting—are no less responsive than legislators from competitive districts. In fact, partly due to the electoral security of their districts, black and Latino legislators are able to pursue their commitment to engage proactively in action to address the collective needs of blacks and Latinos at the same time that they represent their own constituents. Black and Latino legislators are free to stake out positions and bring up perspectives that legislators in electorally competitive districts may not be able to. A legislator such as John Conyers (D-MI) in an urban district is able to advocate for black farmers, for instance. Much research shows, moreover, that no legislator is truly safe from being voted out of office by his or her constituents. Legislators are constantly thinking about the electoral ramifications of their decision making and how their constituents will respond (Fenno 1978; Kingdon 1989; Sulkin 2005). They are also concerned that a challenger may comb through their records and use a stance against them in a future primary or general election (Arnold 1990; Fiorina 1974). Although legislators are free to pursue their commitment to uplift marginalized groups, they are aware that they can be challenged in a primary at any time. For example, Rep. Cynthia McKinney (D-GA) lost her reelection campaign in the Democratic primary when many of her constituents believed that she was spending too much time focusing on foreign policy issues and not enough time addressing issues that were important to the district.

Legislators' Motivations and Strategic Group Uplift

Examining legislators' representational actions in oversight moves us beyond the highly partisan and constrained action of roll-call voting to exploring the impact of the race and ethnicity of legislators in discretionary activities of substantive importance. The majority of early congressional behavior accounts do not systematically examine the effect of race or ethnicity directly or indirectly in structuring legislators' behavior (Achen 1978; Fenno 1978; Fiorina 1974; Kingdon 1989; Miller and Stokes 1963). Many congressional scholars argue that legislators face complex motivations, such as their desire to be reelected, to be loyal to party wishes, and to make good public policy. What is usually missing from these accounts is the importance of racial or ethnic background. Unlike white House members, who can focus their attention solely on attending to the needs of the constituents in their districts, black and Latino legislators must balance the expectations of their constituents with the broader expectation that they represent the needs of all blacks and Latinos. Strategic group uplift motivates legislators to engage in behavior that does not necessarily promote or improve their chances of being reelected. The concept of strategic group uplift provides new insight into why black and Latino legislators are more likely than white legislators to intervene in the oversight of federal policies relating to minority interests.

Personal experiences play a vital role in shaping how all legislators view politics and can affect their decision making and level of advocacy above and beyond party and ideological preferences (Burden 2007; Fenno 2003). In earlier chapters, I showed that black, white, and Latino legislators can be and often are shaped by their personal experiences. These experiences influence the comments that legislators make and the way that they question witnesses at hearings. However, this book advances a theory that goes beyond personal experiences in explaining why black and Latino legislators intervene in agency policymaking. Latino and black legislators differ from white legislators in that black and Latino legislators' personal experience is closely tied to the collective experience of all Latinos and blacks, respectively, while whites' experiences are usually individual in nature.[3] The need to engage in collective action to address many of the issues that plague blacks and Latinos led to the creation of minority caucuses, such as the Congressional Black Caucus and Congressional Hispanic Caucus. These caucuses are charged with representing not just members in their district, but also the interests of blacks and Latinos nationwide. The mission of the caucuses develops out of norms within the black and Latino communities.

Congressional and Bureaucratic Relations

Most of the literature on congressional control of the bureaucracy focuses on the ability of Congress as an institution to influence and, if necessary, restrain the activities of federal agencies charged with implementing laws. Specifically, this literature examines whether Congress engages in active oversight ("police patrols") of federal agency policymaking or whether Congress uses passive controls, such as designing institutional controls ("fire alarms") that allow interest groups to signal when agencies are no longer adhering to congressional preferences (Epstein and O'Halloran 1999; Huber and Shipan 2002; Mayhew 1991; McCubbins and Schwartz 1984; Weingast and Moran 1983). Unlike most research that examines the relationship between Congress and the bureaucracy, this study links

---

[3]This is not to say that whites do not have collective ethnic group identification. For example, Supreme Court Justice Samuel Alito identified with his Italian American heritage. However, white ethnic groups have been able to assimilate in the majority white culture and do not face the same racial and ethnic discrimination encountered by black and Latino legislators. Also, there is no expectation from white ethnics for their group members to advance policies that collectively benefit the group.

efforts by Congress to control the actions of bureaucrats to the political representation of constituent interests by individual legislators. Linking oversight to individual actions provides a greater insight into how oversight is related to substantive representation of constituent interests and how descriptive representation motivates legislators' actions. For example, legislators such as Eva Clayton and John Conyers played a vital role in pressing Congress to weed out discrimination in farm lending programs at the USDA even when the GOP controlled the House. Bounded group uplift has an effect on fire alarm as well as police patrol oversight. When black and Latino farmers sounded the fire alarm about their treatment at the USDA, black and Latino farmers were more likely to pursue their case than white legislators. Even when the farmers are not lobbying legislators, minority legislators continue to pursue their complaints. For over twenty years, John Conyers has used the oversight powers of Congress to continually advocate for fair treatment of black farmers by the USDA.

Limitations of Strategic Group Uplift

There are limitations to what we can expect descriptive representatives to provide in terms of constituent service. The impact of strategic group uplift is not as consistently strong in terms of how much time legislators spend engaging in advocacy for the poor as it is for racial or ethnic issues, but it is still significant.

While black and Latino legislators counteract many of the negative stereotypes about their minority constituents on a variety of issues ranging from affirmative action to welfare reform debates, they do not specifically provide a voice for all members of marginalized groups at all times. Black legislators in districts with a large Hispanic presence may not always spend time advocating for Hispanic interests that they do not have in common with blacks. In the hearings on establishing English only as a common language, black legislators did not intervene to the same degree as they did in a hearing that pertained to repealing bilingual voting requirements.

Scholars who study the intersection of race and gender among marginalized groups argue that racial or ethnic group consciousness is limited on issues that tend to divide the African American community (Cohen 1999; Hancock 2004; Strolovitch 2007). Black legislators' commitment to improve the plight of all blacks is constrained by constituent influence and their desire to be reelected. Even black legislators from the safest districts cannot afford to be active on issues that divide the African American or Latino community. Legislators' decisions to not be as active advocating for the prevention of HIV/AIDS, for instance, are the product of a real constraint the legislators face.

   Moreover, the interplay between strategic group lift and the influence of constituency is difficult to unpack, and most studies of representation, including this one, fail to do so. Are black and Latino legislators motivated to act on minority-interest issues because they are following the preferences of a majority-black or -Latino constituency? Would a white legislator from a majority-minority district behave the same way as a black or Latino legislator from the same district? It is difficult to systematically test this proposition, because few districts meet the criteria. Since 1993, only one white legislator has represented a majority-black district: Steve Cohen (D-TN) represents the district formerly held by Harold Ford Jr. William Jefferson (D-LA), indicted on corruption charges, was defeated by Vietnamese American Republican Anh "Joseph" Cao. Only eight blacks have represented a majority-white district. For Latinos, white legislator Gene Greene in Houston represents predominantly a Hispanic district. Ronald Coleman, a white Democratic legislator from El Paso briefly represented a majority-Hispanic district until he decided not to run for reelection and was replaced by Latino legislator Silvestre Reyes (D-TX). Judy Chu (D-CA), a Chinese American legislator, won a special election in 2009 to represent a majority Hispanic district in the Los Angeles County area that was formerly represented by Latino legislator Hilda Solis (D-CA). Because of the historical exclusion of blacks and Latinos from Congress, most people in the black and Latino community want their representatives to be black or Latino. The paucity of blacks representing majority-white districts suggests that groups prefer electing members from their own racial or ethnic group. The reason may be due to racial fears that whites have about black candidates, or it could be they have greater trust in white candidates. Kingdon (1989) states that it is difficult for constituents to control legislators' actions and monitor their functions. As a result, constituents use elections to select legislators who are most like them (Arnold 1990).

Public Policy Implications

In the United States, where the Census Bureau estimates that racial and ethnic minority groups will constitute a majority of the population by the year 2050, should the diversity of the population be reflected in nation's highest lawmaking body? Racial and ethnic redistricting has done much to increase the number of blacks and Latinos serving in the US House of Representatives. However, there are many who argue that the costs associated with constructing majority-black and -Hispanic districts outweigh the benefits of providing substantive representation to black and Latino constituents (Cameron, Epstein, O'Halloran 1996; Lublin 1997). According to these scholars, the tradeoffs are significant and affect the substantive representation of minority interests, because black constituents who reliably vote for Democrats are removed from some districts to be concentrated in majority-black districts, hurting the election chances of white Democrats. As a result, concentrating blacks in one district leads indirectly to the election of Republican legislators to Congress who usually are not as supportive of minority interests as are Democrats. Increasing the number of descriptive representatives in Congress may harm the Democrats' ability to hold on to a majority and pass legislation that is favorable to minority interests. Black and Latino constituents' policy preferences are consistent with Democratic policy preferences, and thus having a majority-Democrat House leads to policy that is responsive to black and Latino interests. This book has highlighted the strengths that an increase in racial and ethnic diversity brings to oversight in committee deliberations. In 1993–1994, for instance, black committee leaders were able to have a significant impact on welfare reform debates. These legislators were able to keep many of the welfare proposals that would have disproportionately harmed black and Latino constituents from coming to roll-call vote. They also countered many stereotypes and offered alternative viewpoints to the committee deliberations.

Lani Guinier (1995) argues that efforts to increase the number of blacks in office do very little to further the substantive interests of minority groups. Scholars such as Canon (1999) respond directly to Guinier's critique and show that black legislators are just as effective as white legislators in getting their legislation passed through the chamber and eventually signed into law. I show in chapters 4 and 5 that black and Latino legislators have played an instrumental role in ensuring that federal officials as well as fellow congresspersons are enforcing civil rights laws as well as implementing policies that benefit the poor. Guinier, like many scholars, dismisses the importance of the primary function of Congress, which is its oversight and deliberative function. Legislators must spend a great deal of their time ensuring that existing laws are implemented in addition to trying to pass new legislation. One important component of oversight is engaging in the hearings. Part of the job of Congress "is to provide a forum which the demands, interests, opinions, and needs of citizens find articulation" (Sinclair 1989, 2). Black and Latino legislators provide this voice.

In many ways, black and Latino legislators, through the Congressional Black Caucus and Congressional Hispanic Caucus and in their role as lawmakers and overseers, serve as an advocacy group for minority interests. Many scholars have documented the overrepresentation of the voices of the affluent and the middle class in the deliberations and eventual policy output of Congress (Bartels 2008). The bias comes from the overrepresentation of powerful interest groups that lobby for the interests of the rich and powerful and the middle class. The groups representing the poor are fewer in number and vastly underfunded compared to their counterparts. The CBC and CHC subsidize many of the efforts of organized groups that represent racial and ethnic minorities, such as the NAACP and National Council of La Raza. Most studies of organized groups find that these interest groups often subsidize the efforts of the legislators. The increase of black and Latino legislators enables the imbalance of these groups in the pressure group system to be counteracted. Black and Latino legislators provide a voice that fellow Democrats, even liberal Democrats, may not systematically provide, at least as it relates to racial or ethnic issues. With citizen groups declining in resources and membership, these legislators provide forceful representation to groups that would not normally be heard in a complex arena.

This book does not argue that white legislators cannot represent the interests of black and Latino constituents; rather, it highlights the important role that racial and ethnic minorities play in improving the policymaking process through strategic group uplift and by bringing distinctive perspectives to policymaking and congressional oversight. They play a key part in helping Congress formulate policies that consider the viewpoints of marginalized groups who would often otherwise be excluded from the process. As a result of their presence, it is to be hoped that Congress will make better policy decisions than it would make in their absence, and that its deliberations will be sensitive to the needs of minority groups. Perhaps if more racial and ethnic minority legislators had been on the Senate panel handling Judge Sotomayor's confirmation, Senator Tom Coburn (R-OK) would not have told Judge Sotomayor, in a bad Spanish accent, that she had some "splainin to do" in response to an exchange they had concerning gun rights. Coburn used a phrase made popular by the Cuban-American character Ricky Ricardo, played by Desi Arnaz in the television sitcom *I Love Lucy*. Many Latinos, including Rep. Charles González (D-TX), and the National Council of La Raza, thought the senator's comments played into negative stereotypes about Latinos and were inappropriate. If more Latino legislators had been on the panel, then maybe they would have challenged this stereotype and other exchanges that questioned Sotomayor's judicial temperament, which many Latino groups felt played into stereotypes about unruly Latina women.

Is the value of descriptive representation overstated, and could white legislators receive similar information from organized interests or other constituents? Although this is possible, groups that represent racial and ethnic minorities are disadvantaged in the pressure group system. They usually lack resources to provide the perspective and advocacy on every issue in which blacks and Latinos have an interest. Black and Latino legislators in Congress are able to respond to situations and provide input on policies in areas where groups have not had a chance to organize and provide a response.

The infusion of racial and ethnic minorities into the House of Representatives has made Congress more attentive to racial and ethnic issues and to social welfare issues of interest to minorities. Not only have Democratic legislators become more liberal in terms of their voting, but the attention that is devoted to committee hearings on racial and ethnic issues has increased. This shift, by bringing more perspectives into Congress, has made Congress a more legitimate institution in the terms of Robert Dahl's seminal work *Who Governs?: Democracy and Power in an American City*, which explores the people who control governmental institutions that make public policies. Institutions that exclude certain groups are unlikely to be viewed as equitable by those who are excluded from their processes. Political scientists have shown that black constituents living in congressional districts represented by black legislators have more trust in that legislator than do black constituents who live in a district represented by a white legislator (Tate 2003).

Finally, this study points to the importance of investigating representatives' oversight activities alongside their roll-call voting as a true measure of the nature of their representation. To say that engaging in the welfare reform debates or testifying before congressional committees are less important activities than roll-call voting ignores the fact that legislators spend the great bulk of their time engaging in oversight—that these activities are an important part of governance and the policy-making process. The impact of a legislators' race or ethnicity is more likely to show up in these more discretionary activities, moreover, because legislators are less constrained by party when they are engaged in oversight than when they are casting roll-call votes. Evaluating the political representation of constituent interests in activities beyond roll-call voting offers a more comprehensive view of what legislators do and how their actions provide effective representation to various groups, including those who have been historically excluded from the halls of Congress.

Appendix A

Data and Methodology

I USED THE Lexis-Nexis Congressional Universe online database to identify racial/ethnic hearings and social welfare hearings for the 103rd Congress (1993–1995), 104th Congress (1995–1997), and 107th Congress (2001–2003). I used a variety of keyword search terms, such as "civil rights," "race," "black or African American," "Latino or Hispanic," and "discrimination" to identify racial/ethnic hearings, and search such terms as "welfare," "Medicaid," "community development," "poor or poverty," and "affordable housing" for the social welfare issues. Having generated a list of hearings, I, with the help of two research assistants, independently coded the hearings according to whether they addressed racial/ethnic or social welfare issues. For instance, we classified any hearing whose title referred specifically to racial groups such as blacks or Latinos, or to issues that have been traditionally associated with minorities, such as affirmative action and racial profiling, as a racial/ethnic hearing. We followed the same protocol for class-based hearings. Hearings that addressed the needs of low-income individuals, such as Section 8 for affordable housing or Medicaid for health, were coded as social welfare hearings. Since this study is focused only on the representation of black and Latino interests, hearings pertaining to other minorities, such as American Indians and Asian American/Pacific Islanders, were not included. This classification system is similar to Canon's (1999) categorization of minority interests as racial and part-racial, but I separate racial issues from class-based issues.

We identified 59 racial hearings in the 103rd Congress, 20 in the 104th Congress, and 13 in the 107th Congress. For social welfare hearings, we identified 20 in the 103rd Congress, 20 in the 104 Congress, and 28 in the 107 Congress. In order to get a representative sample of the hearings in each issue area, I selected approximately 20 hearings from each of the three Congresses—10 each on social welfare and race/ethnic issues—to code for legislators' interventions. I used the following criteria in selecting the hearings: First, hearings were selected to ensure that the committees' composition included racial or ethnic diversity and that the type of committees conducting the hearings was also diverse. Hearings of all-black or all-white committees were not examined, since they did not contain sufficient racial/ethnic variation for an analysis of racial/ethnic differences. In practice, few committees existed that were not racially or ethnically diverse.

Second, committees that had different' policy jurisdictions were included in the sample. I wanted to ensure, when possible, that no one committee or its membership would dominate the oversight activity recorded. For example, the House Financial Services Subcommittee on Housing and Community Opportunity conducted a great number of hearings on issues that were relevant to minority interests; its membership was urban, and minorities were overrepresented on the committee. Including committees that did not have minority overrepresentation, such as the Department of Transportation, and were not dominated by urban interests, such as the Department of Agriculture, diminished the likelihood of any one committee exercising a disproportionate impact on the results. Finally, we eliminated hearings that were not conducted in Washington, DC, because off-site venues may limit the ability of committee members to intervene and actively engage in oversight.

We had no problem identifying social welfare hearings that met our criteria. We were able to identify only six racial/ethnic hearings for the 107th Congress (2001–2003), however, and nine for 103rd Congress (1993–1995). When the GOP became the majority party after the 1994 election, the number of racial/ethnic hearings decreased dramatically from when the Democrats were in the majority and devoted more attention to racial/ethnic issues. Although the number of hearings devoted to social welfare hearings also declined under GOP control of the House, we were able to identify the required number of social welfare hearings.

Measuring Legislative Interventions

The dependent variable, "legislators' interventions," measures how much time legislators spend directing comments at agency officials, witnesses, or fellow legislators relating to stronger civil rights enforcement or pro-racial policies, either verbally or in writing. To construct the dependent variable, I had a team of five research assistants code transcripts according to the protocol listed in appendix B. First, I, along with two research assistants who served as project managers, coded the transcripts of two test hearings in both the racial/ethnic and social welfare policy areas. The intercoder reliability was 0.96. The project managers then trained other research assistants, who coded the remaining transcripts. The test hearings were not included in the analysis.

The unit of analysis was the statements of individual legislators who were assigned to the committees responsible for holding the hearings and those of legislators who intervened and who were not on the responsible committee. First, research assistants had to determine whether the verbal or written statements of a given legislator were substantive. A substantive

statement expresses some policy preference for increased or reduced government intervention or maintenance of the status quo in the relevant
issue area. If the legislator's statement was substantive, the researcher proceeded to determine the valence of the statement. Once the valence of the
statement was determined, then the researcher would note how many
lines the legislator's statement took up in the transcript. The line count
would be totaled and recorded in a column noting whether the legislator
was in favor, against, neutral toward, or did not express a preference for
the pro-minority position. Tables A.1 and A.2 provide a breakdown of the
distribution of interventions into these categories by congressional term.

TABLE A.1

Distribution of the Number of Interventions for Racial/Ethnic Policies by
Congressional Term

	For	Against	Neutral	Attended but Did Not Speak	No Participation
Committee Members					
107th Congress (2001–2003) n = 174	22% (38)	7% (13)	2% (3)	6% (11)	63% (109)
104th Congress (1995–1997) n = 130	26% (34)	6% (8)	4% (5)	14% (18)	50% (65)
103rd Congress (1993–1995) n = 123	28% (35)	2% (2)	2% (3)	2% (2)	66% (81)
Committee and Noncommittee Members					
107th Congress (2001–2003) n = 192	25% (48)	8% (16)	2% (3)	8% (16)	57% (109)
104th Congress (1995–1997) n = 163	31% (50)	11% (18)	4% (6)	15% (24)	40% (65)
103rd Congress (1993–1995) n = 138	35% (48)	1% (2)	3% (4)	1% (2)	59% (81)

TABLE A.2

Distribution of the Number of Interventions for General Social Welfare Policies
by Congressional Term

	For	Against	Neutral	Attended but Did Not Speak	No Participation
Committee Members					
107th Congress	20%	7%	11%	6%	56%
(2001–2003)	(52)	(18)	(28)	(17)	(149)
n = 264					
104th Congress	40%	17%	0%	8%	35%
(1995–1997)	(78)	(34)	(0)	(15)	(69)
n = 196					
103rd Congress	28%	3%	1%	6%	62%
(1993–1995)	(57)	(6)	(2)	(12)	(124)
n = 201					
Committee and Noncommittee Members					
107th Congress	23%	7%	11%	6%	53%
(2001–2003)	(65)	(20)	(31)	(18)	(149)
n = 283					
104th Congress	41%	19%	.4%	7%	33%
(1995–1997)	(86)	(40)	(1)	(15)	(69)
n = 211					
103rd Congress	31%	6%	1%	6%	57%
(1993–1995)	(66)	(12)	(2)	(12)	(124)
n = 216					

As discussed in chapter 4, there are a variety of ways in which the coding
of the transcripts produces zero observations for legislative interventions.
First, some zero observations are produced by legislators who do not intervene in any oversight activity. These legislators do not write letters or
engage in deliberations advocating a position for or against stronger civil
rights enforcement, nor do they call for vigorous implementation of liberal
social welfare policies. Nonparticipation by these legislators serves to in-
flate the number of zeros in the samples. Table A.1 shows that among
committee members in the racial sample an average of 60 percent of the
observations in all three Congresses were attributed to legislators who did

not participate in any oversight activity by either attending or submitting written statements. The nonparticipation average drops to 52 percent when examining committee and noncommittee members. Table A.2 demonstrates similar results for the social welfare hearings. An average of 51 percent of the observations in all three Congresses was attributed to legislators who did not participate. This nonparticipation average drops slightly to 48 percent for all participants.

Second, zero observations are produced for legislators who attended or wrote letters that were either against or neutral toward stronger civil rights enforcement or the pro-minority position on social welfare policies and for those legislators who attended but did not say anything at all. In the racial sample for committee members in all three Congresses, the average proportion of interventions against or neutral toward stronger enforcement of civil rights was 8 percent, while 7 percent did not say anything. In the social welfare sample for committee members in all three Congresses, by contrast, interventions that were against or neutral toward stronger enforcement of civil rights averaged 13 percent, while 7 percent did not say anything.

Another problem with estimating the models related to repeat observations contained in the data. Because I pooled the intervention information from different committees in the three Congresses that held explicitly racial or social welfare hearings, there were members who served on more than one of the committees and thus appeared more than once in the sample. In the 107th Congress (2001–2003) racial/ethnic sample, for example, Congressman William Clay Jr. (D-MO) served on both the House Financial Services Subcommittee on Housing and Community Opportunity and the full committee of House Government Reform. As a member of each committee, he attended and engaged in the deliberations in each respective hearing. As a result, he appeared twice in the sample. The same happens for legislators who were on the committee but did not attend or engage in the deliberations. Thus, the standard maximum likelihood assumption that all observations are independent was violated. If ordinary estimation procedures had been used without correction for the independence violation, then standard errors for the coefficients would be incorrect (Greene 2000). Essentially, if we had estimated the model without correcting for repeated observations, we would be assuming that Congressman Clay's attendance and intervention at the HUD oversight hearing had no effect on the probability of his attendance and intervention at the House Government Reform's oversight committee relating to racial profiling. To correct for repeat observations, I used clustered standard errors, which relax the independence assumption among observations in the data and produce correct standard errors.

Coding Protocol for Congressional Hearings

(1) Determine type of statement. Statements can include legislators' opening statements, witness testimony, verbal exchanges between legislators and witnesses, verbal or written requests for information by legislators, and letters that are subsequently added to the appendix.

Substantive = 1
Nonsubstantive (administrative/procedural) = 2

Substantive. A substantive statement expresses some policy preference for increased or reduced government intervention or maintenance of the status quo in the relevant issue area. These statements can relate to asking questions to obtain more information about agency policies or programs, criticize or praise the agency on its implementation of policies or programs, or direct the agency to take action. They can also be factual statements in support of a certain point of view or agenda.

Nonsubstantive (administrative/procedural). Administrative or procedural comments are made to help facilitate the meeting, such as "Mr. Baca is now recognized for 10 minutes," "The gentleman's time has expired," or "We are pleased to have Mr. Ryan testifying before the committee." This category also includes statements by participants (legislators, witnesses), such as "Hello" or "I am happy to be here."

(2) Valence. If comments are substantive, then please use the following to assess the valence of the comments.

Comments for = 1

Statements or questions that indicate a policy preference for agency officials to take action for stronger enforcement of existing laws or policies that *minorities favor,* such as stronger enforcement of fair housing laws, elimination of racial profiling, and so forth. For example, in a House subcommittee hearing on HUD enforcement of fair housing laws, members advocating for stronger enforcement wanted HUD officials to get rid of their backlog of unresolved discrimination complaints, dedicate resources to hire more staff to assist in processing complaints, and hire an administrator to head the Fair Housing section at the agency.

Comments against = 2

Includes statements that call for the agency to take stronger action to enforce laws or implement policies that *minorities would not usually favor.*

Comments neutral = 3

This category is intended for members who are clearly on the fence, i.e., where members state that they generally support the agency doing a better job in enforcing or implementing policies but propose an alternative that minorities may or many not favor.

(3) Number of Lines
Number of lines in the hearing that the member is speaking.

(4) Question or Statement

    1 = Statement
    2 = Question

(5) Verbal or Written Statement

    1 = Verbal
    2 = Written

(6) Pages = Page(s) on which the statement appears
Additional Instructions

    (1) Participants may make long statements that may contain both categories—substantive and nonsubstantive. When this occurs, please code the statement in subparts.
    (2) When members show up to make their opening statement and also submit a written copy of the opening statement for the record (which is usually in the appendix), please code only the spoken statements. If the member did not attend, then code their written statement.
    (3) If legislators show up to hearings but do not speak or submit a written statement, then record the frequency of these occurrences.

*Appendix C*_____

Racial/Ethnic Congressional Hearings Coded

Congressional Term (Years)	Subject of Oversight Hearing	House Oversight Committee/Subcommittee
107th Congress (2001–2003)	USDA Civil Rights Program for Farmers	Agriculture/Department Operations, Oversight, Nutrition, and Forestry
	HUD's Enforcement of Fair Housing Law	Financial Services/Housing and Community Opportunity and the Subcommittee on Oversight and Investigations
	DOJ's Enforcement of Civil Rights	Judiciary/Constitution
	U.S. Civil Rights Commission Programs and Activities	Judiciary/Constitution
	Racial Profiling	Government Reform
	U.N. Conference on Racism	International Relations/ International Operations and Human Rights
104th Congress (1995–1997)	Credit Availability to Minority- Owned Small Businesses	Banking, Finance and Urban Affairs/Financial Institutions Supervision, Regulation and Deposit Insurance
	Affirmative Action in Employment	Economic and Educational Opportunities/Employer- Employee Relations
	Equal Employment Opportunity Commission Reforms	Economic and Educational Opportunities/Employer- Employee Relations
	English as a Common Language	Economic and Educational Opportunities/Early Childhood, Youth and Families
	English as the Common Language	Economic and Educational Opportunities/Early Childhood, Youth and Families

Congressional Term (Years)	Subject of Oversight Hearing	House Oversight Committee/Subcommittee
	Repealing Bilingual Voting Requirements	Judiciary/Constitution
	Review of Equal Opportunity Act of 1995	Judiciary/Constitution
	Diversity and Minority Hiring in Intelligence Agencies	Intelligence/Permanent Select Committee on Intelligence
	Human Resource and Diversity	Intelligence/Permanent Select Committee on Intelligence
	Regulatory Barriers to Minority Entrepreneurs	Small Business/Regulation and Paperwork
103th Congress (1993–1995)	Empowering the African-American Community through Financial Institutions and Black Churches	Banking, Finance and Urban Affairs/General Oversight, Investigations, and the Resolution of Failed Financial Institutions
	Equal Employment Opportunity Commission	Education and Labor/Select Education and Civil Rights
	Bilingual Education	Education and Labor/Elementary, Secondary and Vocational Education
	Minority Women and Breast Cancer	Government Operations/Human Resources and Intergovernmental Relations
	AIDS and HIV in the African-American Community	Government Operations/Human Resources and Intergovernmental Relations
	Review of NAFTA's impact on Blue Collar, Minority and Female Employment	Government Operations/Employment, Housing and Aviation
	Review of Federal Measurements of Race and Ethnicity	Post Office and Civil Service/Census Statistics, and Postal Personnel
	Healthcare Opportunities for Minorities	Small Business/Minority Enterprise, Finance and Urban Development
	Hispanic Veterans	Veterans' Affairs/Oversight and Investigations

Appendix D

General Social Welfare Congressional Hearings Coded

Congressional Term (Years)	Subject of Oversight Hearing	House Oversight Committee/Subcommittee
107th Congress (2001–2003)	USDA Domestic Food Distribution Program	Agriculture/Department Operations, Oversight, Nutrition, and Forestry
	Implementation of Welfare Reform	Budget
	Implementation of Welfare Reform	Education and the Workforce/ 21st Century Competitiveness
	Implementation of Welfare Reform	Committee on Ways and Means/ Human Resources
	Affordable Health Care	Energy and Commerce/Health
	Budget Hearing for HUD	Financial Services/Housing and Community Opportunity
	Review of HUD's Community Development Block Grant Program	Financial Services/Housing and Community Opportunity
	Review of Empowerment Zone Programs	Financial Services/Housing and Community Opportunity
	Review of Medicaid Claims Process	Government Reform/Government Efficiency, Financial Management and Intergovernmental Relations
	Affordable Public Transportation	Transportation and Infrastructure/ Highways and Transportation
104th Congress (1995–1997)	Increasing Access of Low and Moderate income Americans to Financial Services	Banking Finance and Urban Affairs/Financial Institutions Supervision, Regulation and Deposit Insurance/Consumer Credit and Insurance

Congressional Term (Years)	Subject of Oversight Hearing	House Oversight Committee/Subcommittee
	HUD's Report on the Federal Home Loan System	Banking, Finance and Urban Affairs/General Oversight, Investigations, and the Resolution of Failed Institutions
	Personal Responsibility and Work Opportunity Act of 1996	Commerce
	Transformation of the Medicaid Program	Commerce/Health and Environment
	Review of HUD's Management of Section 8 Multifamily Housing	Government Reform and Oversight/Human Resources and Intergovernmental Relations
	Review of Consequences of Minimum Wage Increase	Government Reform and Oversight/National Economic Growth, National Resources, and Regulatory Affairs
	Review of HUD	Government Reform and Oversight/Human Resources and Intergovernmental Relations
	Unemployment Insurance Issues	Ways and Means/Human Resources
	Welfare Reform	Ways and Means/Human Resources
	Causes of Poverty	Ways and Means/Human Resources
	Child Care and Child Welfare	Ways and Means/Human Resources and Economic and Educational Opportunities/ Early Childhood, Youth and Families
103th Congress (1993–1995)	Section 8 Housing Assistance Payments Program	Banking, Finance and Urban Affairs/Housing and Community Development
	Work and Responsibility Act of 1994	Education and Labor

(*continued*)

Congressional Term (Years)	Subject of Oversight Hearing	House Oversight Committee/Subcommittee
	Primary Care Services for the Under-served	Energy and Commerce/Health and the Environment
	Medicaid Managed Care	Energy and Commerce/ Oversight and Investigations
	Hunger in America	Small Business/Regulation, Business Opportunities and Technology
	Welfare Reform	Ways and Means/Human Resources
	Trends in Poverty and Family Income	Ways and Means/Human Resources
	Children and Families at Risk	Ways and Means/Human Resources
	Trends in Spending/Caseloads for AFDC	Ways and Means/Human Resources

Appendix E

Likelihood of Intervention for Stronger Enforcement of Civil Rights Policies in the 103rd Congress (1993–1995), First Stage

Explanatory Variables	Committee Members	Committee and Noncommittee Members
Party	.20	−2.40*
	(.60)	(1.46)
Black	2.07+	2.91
	(1.60)	(1.81)
Latino	−1.66	−2.05
	(1.88)	(1.96)
Chair	−23.00**	−24.02**
	(.52)	(.54)
Ranking minority member	−1.31**	−4.73**
	(.63)	(1.44)
% black voting-age population	.03+	−.08*
	(.02)	(.04)
% Hispanic voting-age population	−.01	−.01
	(.02)	(.02)
Median family income	—	—
South	—	—
Electoral safety	—	—
Member of assigned committee	—	3.96**
		(.82)
Constant	2.05**	.85
	(.47)	(.90)
Log pseudo-likelihood	−234.57	−299.87
Wald chi-square (10)	460.74	146.48
	(p<.001)	(p<.001)
Alpha	.35	.34
	(.23)	(.19)
N	123	138

Robust standard errors are in parentheses.
*Statistically significant at .05 level, one-tailed test.
**Statistically significant at .01 level, one-tailed test.
+Statistically significant at .10 level, one-tailed test.

Appendix F

Likelihood of Intervention for Stronger Enforcement of Civil Rights Policies in the 104th Congress (1995–1997), First Stage

Explanatory Variables	Committee Members	Committee and Noncommittee Members
Party	−.73	−1.28**
	(.69)	(.58)
Black	.15	.16
	(1.43)	(1.22)
Latino	1.23	−.71
	(1.23)	(.96)
Chair	−.65	−.92
	(.71)	(.73)
Ranking minority member	−2.01**	−1.31**
	(.76)	(.63)
Latino ranking minority member	—	—
% black voting-age population	−.01	−.01
	(.03)	(.03)
% Hispanic voting-age population	−.03*	−.01
	(.02)	(.02)
Median family income	—	—
South	—	—
Electoral safety	—	—
Member of assigned committee	—	.75*
		(.45)
Constant	2.07**	1.49**
	(.48)	(.44)
Log pseudo-likelihood	−227.95	−328.35
Wald chi-square (11)	297.12	65.21
	(p<.001)	(p<.001)
Alpha	.19	.28
	(.22)	(.16)
N	130	163

Robust standard errors are in parentheses.
*Statistically significant at .05 level, one-tailed test.
**Statistically significant at .01 level, one-tailed test.
+Statistically significant at .10 level, one-tailed test.

Appendix G

Likelihood of Intervention for Stronger Enforcement of Civil Rights Policies in the 107th Congress (2001–2003), First Stage

Explanatory Variables	Committee Members	Committee and Noncommittee Members
Party	−1.95**	−2.05**
	(.61)	(.60)
Black	−2.60**	−2.86**
	(1.10)	(1.07)
Latino	−.69	−.54
	(1.45)	(1.36)
Chair	−3.06**	−3.15**
	(.82)	(.85)
Ranking minority member	—	—
Black ranking minority member	—	—
% black voting-age population	2.13	3.21+
	(2.20)	(2.28)
% Hispanic voting-age population	.20	−.45
	(1.95)	(1.98)
Median family income	—	—
South	—	—
Electoral safety	—	—
Member of assigned committee	—	.61
	(.59)	
Constant	2.87**	2.29**
	(.53)	(.71)
Log pseudo-likelihood	−256.31	−318.05
Wald chi-square (11)	131.62	145.15
	(p<.01)	(p<.01)
Alpha	.30	−1.22
	(.19)	(.52)
N	174	192

Robust standard errors are in parentheses.

*Statistically significant at .05 level, one-tailed test.

**Statistically significant at .01 level, one-tailed test.

+Statistically significant at .10 level, one-tailed test.

Likelihood of Intervention for General Social Welfare Policies in the 103rd Congress (1993–1995), First Stage

Explanatory Variables	Committee Members	Committee and Noncommittee Members
Party	−.65+	−.72+
	(.41)	(.40)
Black	−1.61+	−1.48+
	(1.08)	(1.03)
Latino	−.31	−.95
	(1.06)	(1.10)
Chair	−1.69**	−1.87**
	(.49)	(.53)
Black chair	—	—
Ranking minority member	−1.31**	−1.46**
	(.63)	(.64)
% black voting-age population	.03+	.03+
	(.02)	(.02)
% Hispanic voting-age population	−.02	−.01
	(.02)	(.02)
Median family income	—	—
South	—	—
Electoral safety	—	—
Member of assigned committee	—	1.57**
		(.54)
Constant	2.22*	.07**
	(.99)	(.61)
Log pseudo-likelihood	−410.69	−467.53
Wald chi-square (11)	242.02	272.13
	(p<.001)	(p<.001)
Alpha	.39	.41
	(.22)	(.20)
N	201	216

Robust standard errors are in parentheses.
*Statistically significant at .05 level, one-tailed test.
**Statistically significant at .01 level, one-tailed test.
+Statistically significant at .10 level, one-tailed test.

Appendix I

Likelihood of Intervention for General Social Welfare Policies in the 104th Congress (1995–1997), First Stage

Explanatory Variables	Committee Members	Committee and Noncommittee Members
Party	−1.08**	−1.23**
	(.39)	(.38)
Black	−.92*	−.99*
	(.51)	(.49)
Latino	—	—
Chair	−1.53**	−1.63**
	(.72)	(.72)
Ranking minority member	−1.25*	−1.16*
	(.71)	(.66)
% black voting-age population	.02	.02*
	(.01)	(.01)
% Hispanic voting-age population	−.00	−.00
	(.01)	(.01)
Median family income	—	—
South	—	—
Electoral safety	—	—
Member of assigned committee	—	.80*
		(.50)
Constant	.97**	1.01**
	(.25)	(.25)
Log pseudo-likelihood	−519.88	−564.43
Wald chi-square (10)	604.91	142.20
	(p<.001)	(p<.001)
Alpha	.65	.63
	(.16)	(.15)
N	196	211

Robust standard errors are in parentheses.
*Statistically significant at .05 level, one-tailed test.
**Statistically significant at .01 level, one-tailed test.
+Statistically significant at .10 level, one-tailed test.

Likelihood of Intervention for General Social Welfare
Policies in the 107th Congress (2001–2003), First Stage

Explanatory Variables	Committee Members	Committee and Noncommittee Members
Party	−1.61**	−1.32**
	(.42)	(.37)
Black	−1.10+	−1.13*
	(.70)	(.69)
Latino	—	—
Chair	−2.05**	−.90
	(.78)	(1.06)
Ranking minority member	−1.23*	−1.27*
	(.60)	(.60)
% black voting-age population	.15	.15
	(1.66)	(1.60)
% Hispanic voting-age population	−.80	−.70
	(1.01)	(.95)
Median family income	—	—
South	—	—
Electoral safety	—	—
Member of assigned committee	—	2.39**
		(.67)
Constant	2.80**	.13**
	(.40)	(.69)
Log pseudo-likelihood	−359.92	−444.90
Wald chi-square (10)	56.07	19.70
	(p<.001)	(p<.05)
Alpha	.41	.45
	(.20)	(.14)
N	264	283

Robust standard errors are in parentheses.
*Statistically significant at .05 level, one-tailed test.
**Statistically significant at .01 level, one-tailed test.
+Statistically significant at .10 level, one-tailed test.

References

Aberbach, Joel. 1990. *Keeping a Watchful Eye: The Politics of Congressional Oversight.* Washington, DC: Brookings Institution.

Achen, Christopher H. 1978. "Measuring Representation." *American Political Science Review* 22: 475–510.

Amer, Mildred. 2004. *Membership of the 108th Congress: A Profile.* Washington, DC: Congressional Research Service.

Arnold, R. Douglas. 1990. *The Logic of Congressional Action.* New Haven, CT: Yale University Press.

Bartels, Larry M. 2008. *Unequal Democracy: The Political Economy of the New Gilded Age.* Princeton, NJ: Princeton University Press.

Bauer, Raymond, Ithiel de Sola Pool, and Lewis Anthony Dexter. 1963. *American Business and Public Policy.* New York: Atherton Press.

Berry, Jeffrey M. 1999. *The New Liberalism: The Rising Power of Citizen Groups.* Washington, DC: Brookings Institution Press.

Bibby, John F. 1968. "Congress' Neglected Function." In Melvin R. Laird, ed., *The Republican Papers.* New York: Doubleday Anchor, 1968.

Bratton, Kathleen A. 2006. "The Behavior and Success of Latino Legislators: Evidence from the States," *Social Science Quarterly* 87: 1136–1157.

Bratton, Kathleen A., and Kerry L. Haynie. 1999. "Agenda-Setting and Legislative Success in State Legislatures: The Effects of Gender and Race." *Journal of Politics* 61: 658–79.

Burden, Barry C. 2007. *Personal Roots of Representation.* Princeton, NJ: Princeton University Press.

Calhoun-Brown, Allison. 1996. "African American Churches and Political Mobilization: The Psychological Impact of Organizational Resources." *Journal of Politics* 58: 935–53.

Cameron, Charles, David Epstein, and Sharyn O'Halloran. 1996. "Do Majority-Minority Districts Maximize Substantive Black Representation in Congress?" *American Political Science Review* 90: 794–812.

Canon, David T. 1999. *Race, Redistricting, and Representation: The Unintended Consequences of Black Majority Districts.* Chicago: University of Chicago Press.

Carmines, Edward G., and James A. Stimson. 1989. *Issue Evolution : Race and the Transformation of American Politics.* Princeton, NJ: Princeton University Press.

Carpenter, Daniel P. 2001. *The Forging of Bureaucratic Autonomy: Reputations, Networks, and Policy Innovation in Executive Agencies, 1862–1928.* Princeton, NJ: Princeton University Press.

Casellas, Jason P. 2010. *Latino Representation in State Houses and Congress.* New York: Cambridge University Press.

Chavez, Maria L. 2004. "Overview." In Sharon A. Navarro and Armando X. Mejia, eds., *Latino Americans and Political Participation: A Reference Handbook,* 1–56. Santa Barbara, CA: ABC-CLIO, Inc.

Clay, Willam L. 1993. *Just Permanent Interests: Black Americans in Congress 1870–1992*. New York: Amistad Press, Inc.

Cobb, Michael D., and Jeffery A. Jenkins. 2001. "Race and the Representation of Blacks' Interests During Reconstruction," *Political Research Quarterly* 54: 181–204.

Cohen, Cathy J. 1999. *The Boundaries of Blackness: AIDS and the Breakdown of Black Politics*. Chicago: University of Chicago Press.

Conover, Pamela J. 1984. "The Influence of Group Identifications on Political Perception and Evaluation," *Journal of Politics* 46: 760–85.

Cox, Gary W., and Mathew D. McCubbins. 2005. *Setting the Agenda: Responsible Party Government in the U.S. House of Representatives*. New York: Cambridge University Press.

Dahl, Robert A. 1961. *Who Governs?: Democracy and Power in an American City*. New Haven, CT: Yale University Press.

Dawson, Michael C. 2001. *Black Visions: Roots of Contemporary African American Ideology*. Chicago: University of Chicago Press.

———. 1994. *Behind the Mule: Race and Class in African-American Politics*. Princeton, NJ: Princeton University Press.

Dovi, Suzanne. 2002. "Preferable Descriptive Representatives: Will Just Any Woman, Black, or Latino Do?" *American Political Science Review* 96: 729–43.

DuBois, W. E. B. 1982 (1903). *The Souls of Black Folk*. New York: Bantam Books.

Duffin, Diane. 2003. "Explaining Participation in Congressional Oversight Hearings." *American Politics Research* 31: 455–80.

Epstein, David, and Sharyn O'Halloran. 1999. *Delegating Powers: A Transaction Cost Politics Approach to Policy Making under Separate Powers*. Cambridge: Cambridge University Press.

Erikson, Robert S. 1978. "Constituency Opinion and Congressional Behavior: A Reexamination of the Miller-Stokes Representation Data." *American Journal of Political Science* 22: 511–35.

Eulau, Heinz, and Paul D. Karps. 1977. "The Puzzle of Representation: Specifying Components of Responsiveness." *Legislative Studies Quarterly* 2: 233–54.

Fenno, Richard F. 2003. *Going Home: Black Representatives and Their Constituents*. Chicago: University of Chicago Press.

———. 1978. *Home Style: House Members in Their Districts*. New York: Addison-Wesley Educational Publishers, Inc.

Fiorina, Morris. 1974. *Representatives, Roll Calls, and Constituencies*. Lexington, MA: Lexington Books.

Foner, Eric. 1988. *Reconstruction: America's Unfinished Revolution, 1863–1877*. New York: Harper & Row Publishers.

Foreman, Christopher H. 1988. *Signals from the Hill: Congressional Oversight and the Challenge of Social Regulation*. New Haven, CT: Yale University Press.

Gamble, Katrina L. 2007. "Black Political Representation: An Examination of Legislative Activity Within U.S. House Committees." *Legislative Studies Quarterly* 32: 421–47.

Garcia Bedolla, Lisa. 2009. *Latino Politics*. Cambridge: Polity Press.

Gay, Claudine. 2001. "The Effect of Black Congressional Representation on Political Participation." *American Political Science Review* 95: 589–602.

Gerber, Elisabeth R., Rebecca Morton, and Thomas Rietz. 1998. "Minority Representation in Multimember Districts." *American Political Science Review* 92: 127–44.

Gillette, William. 1979. *Retreat from Reconstruction, 1869–1879*. Baton Rouge: Louisiana State University Press.

Griffin, John D., and Brian Newman. 2008. *Minority Report: Evaluating Political Equality in America*. Chicago: University of Chicago Press.

Grofman, Bernard, and Lisa Handley. 1989. "Minority Population and Black and Hispanic Congressional Success in the 1970s and 1980s." *American Politics Quarterly* 17: 436–45.

Grose, Christian. 2011. *Congress in Black and White: Race and Representation in Washington and at Home*. Cambridge: Cambridge University Press.

———. 2003. "Beyond the Vote: A Theory of Black Representation in Congress." Paper delivered at the University of Rochester's Conference on New Perspectives on the Study of Race and Political Representation, Rochester, New York.

Grosfoguel, Ramon. 2003. *Colonial Subjects: Puerto Ricans in a Global Perspective*. Berkeley: University of California Press.

Guinier, Lani. 1995. *The Tyranny of the Majority: Fundamental Fairness in Representative Democracy*. New York: Free Press.

Gurin, Patricia, Shirley Hatchett, and James S. Jackson. 1989. *Hope and Independence: Blacks' Response to Electoral and Party Politics*. New York: Russell Sage Foundation.

Hall, Richard L. 1996. *Participation in Congress*. New Haven, CT: Yale University Press.

Hall, Richard L., and C. Lawrence Evans. 1990. "The Power of Subcommittees." *Journal of Politics* 52: 335–55.

Hall, Richard L., and Bernard Grofman. 1990. "The Committee Assignment Process and the Conditional Nature of Committee Bias." *American Political Science Review* 84: 1149–66.

Hall, Richard L., and Colleen Heflin. 1994. "The Color of Representation in Congress." Paper delivered at the Annual Meeting of the Midwest Political Science Association, Chicago, Illinois.

Hall, Richard L., and Kris Miler. 2000. "Interest Group Subsidies to Legislative Overseers." Paper delivered at the Annual Meeting of the American Political Science Association, Atlanta, Georgia.

Hamilton, Dona C., and Charles V. Hamilton. 1997. *The Dual Agenda: Race and Social Welfare Policies of Civil Rights Organizations*. New York: Columbia University Press.

Hamilton, Lawrence C. 2004. *Statistics with Stata: Updated for Version 8*. Belmont, CA: Brooks/Cole/Thompson Learning, Inc.

Hancock, Ange-Marie. 2004. *The Politics of Disgust: The Public Identity of the Welfare Queen*. New York: New York University Press.

Haynie, Kerry L. 2001. *African American Legislators in the American States*. New York: Columbia University Press.

Hero, Rodney E. 1992. *Latinos and the U.S. Political System: Two-Tiered Pluralism*. Philadelphia: Temple University Press.

Hero, Rodney E., and Caroline J. Tolbert. 1995. "Latinos and Substantive Representation in the U.S. House of Representatives: Direct, Indirect, or Nonexistent?" *American Journal of Political Science* 39: 640–52.

Hoffman, Abraham. 1974. *Unwanted Mexican Americans in the Great Depression: Reparations Pressures 1929–1939.* Tucson: The University of Arizona Press.

Huber, Gregory A. 2007. *The Craft of Bureaucratic Neutrality : Interests and Influence in Governmental Regulation of Occupational Safety.* Cambridge: Cambridge University Press.

Huber, John, and Charles Shipan. 2002. *Deliberate Discretion: The Institutional Foundations of Bureaucratic Autonomy.* New York: Cambridge University Press.

Hutchings, Vincent L. 1998. "Issue Salience and Support for Civil Rights Legislation Among Southern Democrats." *Legislative Studies Quarterly* 23: 521–44.

Hutchings, Vincent L., Harwood K. McClerking, and Guy-Uriel Charles. 2004. "Congressional Representation of Black Interests: Recognizing the Importance of Stability." *Journal of Politics* 66: 450–68.

Jackson, John E., and David C. King. 1989. "Private Interests, Public Goods, and Representation." *American Political Science Review* 83: 1143–64.

James, Scott, and Brian Lawson. 1999. "The Political Economy of Voting Rights Enforcement in America's Gilded Age: Electoral College Competition, Partisan Commitment, and the Federal Election Law." *American Political Science Review* 93: 115–31.

Kathlene, Lyn. 1994. "Power and Influence in State Legislative Policymaking: The Interaction of Gender and Position in Committee Hearing Debates." *American Political Science Review* 88: 560–76.

Kinder, Donald R., and Lynn M. Sanders. 1996. *Divided by Color: Racial Politics and Democratic Ideals.* Chicago: University of Chicago Press.

Kingdon, John W. 1989. *Congressmen's Voting Decisions.* Ann Arbor: University of Michigan Press.

Kousser, J. Morgan. 1974. *The Shaping of Southern Politics: Suffrage Restriction and the Establishment of the One-Party South, 1880–1910.* New Haven: Yale University Press.

Lawrence, Eric D., Forrest Maltzman, and Steven S. Smith. 2006. "Who Wins? Party Effects in Legislative Voting." *Legislative Studies Quarterly* 31: 33–69.

Leal, David L. 2007. "Latino Public Opinion: Does It Exist?" In Rodolfo Espino, David L. Leal, and Kenneth J. Meier, eds. *Latino Politics: Identity, Mobilization, and Representation,* 27–43. Charlottesville: University of Virginia Press.

Lieberman, Robert C. 1998. *Shifting the Color Line: Race and the American Welfare State.* Cambridge, MA: Harvard University Press.

Long, J. Scott, and Jeremy Freese. 2003. *Regression Models for Categorical Dependent Variables Using Stata.* Rev. ed.. College Station, TX: Stata Corporation.

Lublin, David. 1999. "Racial Redistricting and African-American Representation: A Critique of 'Do Majority-Minority Districts Maximize Substantive Black Representation in Congress?'" *American Political Science Review* 93: 183–86.

———. 1997. *The Paradox of Representation: Racial Gerrymandering and Minority Interests in Congress.* Princeton, NJ: Princeton University Press.

Maltzman, Forrest, and Lee Sigelman. 1996. "The Politics of Talk: Unconstrained Floor Time in the U.S. House of Representatives." *Journal of Politics* 58: 819–30.

Mansbridge, Jane. 2003. "Rethinking Representation." *American Political Science Review* 97: 515–28.

———. 1999. "Should Blacks Represent Blacks and Women Represent Women? A Contingent Yes." *Journal of Politics* 61: 628–57.

Massey, Douglas S., and Nancy A. Denton. 1993. *American Apartheid: Segregation and the Making of the Underclass.* Cambridge, MA: Harvard University
Press.

Mayhew, David. 1991. *Divided We Govern: Party Control, Lawmaking, and Investigations, 1946–1990.* New Haven, CT: Yale University Press.

———. 1974. *Congress: The Electoral Connection.* New Haven, CT: Yale University
Press.

McClain, Paula D. 1993. "The Changing Dynamics of Urban Politics: Black and
Hispanic Municipal Employment—Is There Competition?" *Journal of Politics*
55: 399–414.

McClain, Paula D., and Albert K. Karnig. 1990. "Black and Hispanic Socioeconomic and Political Competition." *American Political Science Review* 84: 535–45.

McClerking, Harwood K. 2001. "We Are in This Together: The Origins and Maintenance of Black Common Fate Perceptions." PhD diss., University of Michigan
Libraries.

McClerking, Harwood, and Eric L. McDaniel. 2005. "Belonging and Doing: Political Churches and Black Political Participation." *Political Psychology* 26: 721–33.

McCubbins, Mathew D., Roger G. Noll, and Barry R. Weingast. 1987. "Administrative Procedures as Instruments of Political Control." *Journal of Law, Eco-
nomics, and Organization* 3 (2): 243–77.

McCubbins, Mathew D., and Thomas Schwartz. 1984. "Congressional Oversight
Overlooked: Police Patrols Versus Fire Alarms." *American Journal of Political
Science* 28: 165–69.

McKenzie, Brian D. 2004. "Religious Social Networks, Indirect Mobilization, and
African-American Political Participation." *Political Research Quarterly* 57: 621–32.

Miler, Kristina C. 2010. *Constituency Representation in Congress: A View from Capitol
Hill.* Cambridge: Cambridge University Press.

Miller, Arthur H., Patricia Gurin, Gerald Gurin and Oksana Malanchuk. 1981.
"Group Consciousness and Political Participation." *American Journal of Political Science* 25: 494–511.

Miller, Warren E., and Donald E. Stokes. 1963. "Constituency Influence in Congress." *American Political Science Review* 57: 45–56.

Minta, Michael D. 2009. "Legislative Oversight and the Substantive Representation of Black and Latino Interests in Congress." *Legislative Studies Quarterly*
34: 193–218.

Navarro, Sharon A., and Armando X. Mejia, eds. *Latino Americans and Political
Participation: A Reference Handbook.* Santa Barbara, CA: ABC-CLIO, Inc.

Pennock, J. Roland. 1979. *Democratic Political Theory.* Princeton, NJ: Princeton
University Press.

Phillips, Anne. 1995. *The Politics of Presence.* Oxford: Oxford University Press.

Pitkin, Hanna F. 1967. *The Concept of Representation.* Berkeley: University of California Press.

Ogul, Morris. 1976. *Congress Oversees the Bureaucracy: Studies in Legislative Supervision.* Pittsburgh: University of Pittsburgh Press.

Oliver, Melvin L., and Thomas M. Shapiro. 1995. *Black Wealth, White Wealth: A
New Perspective on Racial Inequality.* New York: Routledge.

Poole, Keith, and Howard Rosenthal. 1997. *Congress: A Political-Economic History of Roll-Call Voting.* Oxford: Oxford University Press.

Reeves, Keith. 1997. *Voting Hopes or Fears: White Voters, Black Candidates and Racial Politics in America*. New York: Oxford University Press.

Reingold, Beth. 2000. *Representing Women: Sex, Gender, and Legislative Behavior in Arizona and California*. Chapel Hill: University of North Carolina Press.

Rodrigues, Helen A., and Gary Segura. 2007. "A Place at the Lunch Counter: Latinos, African Americans, and the Dynamics of American Race Politics." In Rodolfo Espino, David L. Leal, and Kenneth J. Meier, eds., *Latino Politics: Identity, Mobilization, and Representation*, 27–43.

Sanchez, Gabriel R. 2006. "The Role of Group Consciousness in Latino Public Opinion." *Political Research Quarterly* 59: 435–46.

Schmidt, Ronald Sr. 1997. "Latinos and Language Policy: The Politics of Culture." In F. Chris Garcia, ed., *Pursuing Power: Latinos and the Political System*, 343–67. South Bend, IN: University of Notre Dame Press.

Sinclair, Barbara. 1989. *The Transformation of the U.S. Senate*. Baltimore: The Johns Hopkins University Press.

Sinclair-Chapman, Valeria. 2003. "Transforming Politics: Advocating Black Interests Through Bill Sponsorship." Paper delivered at the University of Rochester's Conference on New Perspectives on the Study of Race and Political Representation, Rochester, New York.

Smith, Robert C., and Richard Seltzer. 2000. *Contemporary Controversies and the American Racial Divide*. Lanham, MD: Rowman and Littlefield Publishers, Inc.

Stokes, Atiya Kai. 2003. "Latino Group Consciousness and Political Participation." *American Politics Research* 31: 361–78.

Strolovitch, Dara Z. 2007. *Affirmative Advocacy: Race, Class, and Gender in Interest Group Politics*. Chicago: University of Chicago Press.

Sulkin, Tracy. 2005. *Issue Politics*. New York: Cambridge University Press.

Swain, Carol M. 1993. *Black Faces, Black Interests: The Representation of African Americans in Congress*: Cambridge, MA: Harvard University Press.

Swers, Michele L. 2002. *The Difference Women Make : The Policy Impact of Women in Congress*. Chicago: University of Chicago Press.

———. 1998. "Are Women More Likely to Vote for Women's Issue Bills than Their Male Colleagues?" *Legislative Studies Quarterly* 23: 435–48.

Tate, Katherine. 2003. *Black Faces in the Mirror: African Americans and Their Representatives in the U.S. Congress*. Princeton, NJ: Princeton University Press.

———. 1993. *From Protest to Politics: The New Black Voters in American Elections*. Cambridge, MA: Harvard University Press.

Thernstrom, Abigail. 1987. *Whose Votes Count? Affirmative Action and Minority Voting Rights*. Cambridge, MA: Harvard University Press.

US Congress. House. Committee on Agriculture. 2002. *U.S. Department of Agriculture's Civil Rights Program for Farm Program Participants: Hearing before the Subcommittee on Department Operations, Oversight, Nutrition, and Forestry*. 107th Cong., 2nd sess., Sept. 25.

———. 2001. *USDA Domestic Food Distribution Programs: Hearing before the Subcommittee on Department Operations, Oversight, Nutrition, and Forestry*. 107th Cong., 1st sess., Apr. 3.

———. Committee on Banking, Finance and Urban Affairs. 1994. *Availability of Credit to Minority-Owned Small Businesses: Hearing before the Subcommittee on*

Financial Institutions Supervision, Regulation and Deposit Insurance. 104th Cong., 2nd sess., Oct. 6.

———. 1994. *Ways of Increasing Access of Low- and Moderate-Income Americans to Financial Services: Joint Hearing before the Subcommittee on Financial Institutions Supervision, Regulation and Deposit Insurance and Subcommittee on Consumer Credit and Insurance.* 104th Cong., 2nd sess., Aug. 11.

———. 1994. *Financial Institutions and Black Churches: Forging a Partnership to Empower the African-American Community: Hearing before the Subcommittee on General Oversight, Investigations, and the Resolution of Failed Financial Institutions.* 103rd Cong., 2nd sess., Sept. 16.

———. 1994. *HUD's Report to Congress on the Federal Home Loan System: Hearing before the Subcommittee on General Oversight, Investigations, and the Resolution of Failed Financial Institutions.* 104th Cong., 2nd sess., May 24.

———. 1993. *Section 8 Housing Assistance Payments Program: Hearing before the Subcommittee on Housing and Community Development.* 103rd Cong., 1st sess., Nov. 3.

———. Committee on the Budget. 2001. *Making Ends Meet: Challenges Facing Working Families in America. Hearing before the Committee on the Budget.* 107th Cong., 2nd sess., Aug. 1.

———. Committee on Commerce. 1996. *Personal Responsibility and Work Opportunity Act of 1996: Hearing before the Committee on Commerce.* 104th Cong., 2nd sess., June 11.

———. 1995. *Transformation of the Medicaid Program, Part 3: Hearing before the Subcommittee on Health and Environment.* 104th Cong., 1st sess., July 26 and Aug. 1.

———. Committee on Economic and Educational Opportunities. 1995. *Hearings on Affirmative Action in Employment: Hearing before the Subcommittee on Employer-Employee Relations.* 104th Cong., 1st sess., Mar. 24 and May 2.

———. 1995. *Hearing on Equal Employment Opportunity Commission (EEOC) Administrative Reforms/Case Processing: Hearing before the Subcommittee on Employer-Employee Relations.* 104th Cong., 1st sess., May 23.

———. 1995. *Hearing on English as a Common Language: Hearing before the Subcommittee on Early Childhood, Youth and Families.* 104th Cong., 1st sess., Oct. 18.

———. 1995. *Hearing on English as the Common Language: Hearing before the Subcommittee on Early Childhood, Youth and Families.* 104th Cong., 1st sess., Nov. 1.

———. Committee on Education and Labor. 1994. *Hearing on H.R. 4605, Work and Responsibility Act of 1994: Hearing before the Committee on Education and Labor.* 103rd Cong., 2nd sess., Aug. 2.

———. 1993. *Oversight Hearing on the Equal Employment Opportunity Commission: Hearing before the Subcommittee on Select Education and Civil Rights.* 103rd Cong., 1st sess., July 27.

———. 1993. *Hearing on Bilingual Education: Hearing before the Subcommittee on Elementary, Secondar y, and Vocational Education.* 103rd Cong., 1st sess., July 22.

———. Committee on Education and the Workforce. 2001. *Welfare Reform: An Examination of Effects: Hearing before the Subcommittee on 21st Century Competitiveness of the Committee on Education and the Workforce.* 107th Cong., 1st sess., Sept. 20.

———. Committee on Energy and Commerce. 2002. *The Uninsured and Afford-able Health Coverage: Hearing before the Subcommittee on Health of the Commit-tee on Energy and Commerce.* 107th Cong., 2nd sess., Feb. 28.

———. 1993. *Primary Care Services for the Underserved: Hearing before the Sub-committee on Health and the Environment.* 103rd Cong., 1st sess., June 9.

———. 1993. *Medicaid Managed Care: Hearing before the Subcommittee on Over-sight and Investigations.* 103rd Cong., 1st sess., Mar. 17.

———. Committee on Financial Services. 2002. *Fighting Discrimination Against the Disabled and Minorities Through Fair Housing Enforcement: Joint Hearing before the Subcommittee on Housing and Community Development and the Sub-committee on Oversight and Investigations.* 107th Cong., 2nd sess., June 25.

———. 2002. *The Proposed Budget of the Department of Housing and Urban De-velopment for Fiscal Year 2003: Hearing before the Subcommittee on Housing and Community Opportunity.* 107th Cong., 2nd sess., Feb. 13.

———. 2002. *Review of the Community Development Block Grant Program: Hear-ing before the Subcommittee on Housing and Community Opportunity.* 107th Cong., 2nd sess., Mar. 14.

———. 2002. *Review of the Current Status of Empowerment Zones and Renewal Communities: Hearing before the Subcommittee on Housing and Community Op-portunity.* 107th Cong., 2nd sess., April 10.

———. Committee on Government Operations. 1994. *Minority Women and Breast Cancer: Hearing before the Human Resources and Intergovernmental Relations Subcommittee.* 103rd Cong., 2nd sess., October 4.

———. 1994. *AIDS and HIV Infection in the African-American Community: Hearing before the Human Resources and Intergovernmental Relations Subcom-mittee.* 103rd Cong., 2nd sess., Sept. 16.

———. 1993. *NAFTA: A Negative Impact on Blue Collar, Minority, and Female Employment?: Hearing before the Employment, Housing and Aviation Subcom-mittee.* 103rd Cong., 1st sess., Nov. 10.

———. Committee on Government Reform. 2001. *Benefits of Audio-Visual Tech-nology in Addressing Racial Profiling: Hearing before the Committee on Govern-ment Reform.* 107th Cong., 1st sess., July 19.

———. 2002. *Medicaid Claims: Who's Watching the Money?: Hearing before the Subcommittee on Government Efficiency, Financial Management and Intergov-ernmental Relations of the Committee on Government Reform.* 107th Cong., 2nd sess., June 13.

———. Committee on Government Reform and Oversight. 1996. *Management of HUD's Section 8 Multifamily Housing Portfolio: Hearing before the Subcom-mittee on Human Resources and Intergovernmental Relations.* 104th Cong., 2nd sess., July 30.

———. 1996. *The Pitfalls of a Minimum Wage Increase: Hearing before the Sub-committee on National Economic Growth, National Resources, and Regulatory Affairs.* 104th Cong., 2nd sess., May 14.

———. 1995. *Oversight Hearing on the Department of Housing and Urban Devel-opment: Hearing before the Subcommittee on Human Resources and Intergovern-mental Relations.* 104th Cong., 1st sess., Feb. 13 and 22.

———. Committee on International Relations. 2001. *Discussion on the U.N. World Conference against Racism.* 107th Cong., 1st sess., July 31.

————. Committee on the Judiciary. 1996. *Bilingual Voting Requirements Repeal Act: Hearing before the Subcommittee on the Constitution.* 104th Cong., 2nd sess., April 18.

————. 2002. *Civil Rights Commission: Hearing before the Subcommittee on the Constitution.* 107th Cong., 2nd sess., April 11.

————. 2002. *Civil Rights Division of the U.S. Department of Justice: Hearing before the Subcommittee on the Constitution.* 107th Cong., 2nd sess., June 25.

————. 1995. *Equal Opportunity Act of 1995: Hearing before the Subcommittee on the Constitution.* 104th Cong., 1st sess., Dec. 7.

————. Committee on Post Office and Civil Service. 1993. *Review of Federal Measurements of Race and Ethnicity: Hearings before the Subcommittee on Census, Statistics, and Postal Personnel.* 103rd Cong., 1st sess., Apr. 14, June 30, July 29, and Nov. 3.

————. Committee on Small Business. 1995. *Regulatory Barriers to Minority Entrepreneurs: Hearing before the Subcommittee on Regulation and Paperwork.* 104th Cong., 1st sess., June 7.

————. 1994. *Hunger in America: Public and Private Responses: Hearing before the Subcommittee on Regulation, Business Opportunities, and Technology.* 103rd Cong., 2nd sess., Dec. 21.

————. 1993. *Healthcare Opportunities for Minorities: Hearing before the Subcommittee on Minority Enterprise, Finance, and Urban Development.* 103rd Cong., 1st sess., Nov. 9.

————. Committee on Transportation and Infrastructure. 2002. *How Transit Serves and Benefits U.S. Communities: Hearing before the Subcommittee on Highways and Transportation.* 107th Cong., 2nd sess., Apr. 17.

————. Committee on Veterans' Affairs. 1994. *Hispanic Veterans: Contributions to the Nation and Community, Receipt of Federal Veterans' Benefits and Related Issues: Hearing before the Subcommittee on Oversight and Investigations.* 103rd Cong., 2nd sess., Sept. 28.

————. Committee on Ways and Means. 2002. *Implementation of Welfare Reform Work Requirements and Time Limits: Hearings before the Subcommittee on Human Resources.* 107th Cong., 2nd sess., Mar. 7.

————. 1996. *Unemployment Insurance Issues: Hearing before the Subcommittee on Human Resources.* 104th Cong., 2nd sess., July 11.

————. 1996. *Welfare Reform: Hearings before the Subcommittee on Human Resources.* 104th Cong., 2nd sess., May 22 and 23.

————. 1996. *Causes of Poverty, with a Focus on Out-of-Wedlock Births: Hearings before the Subcommittee on Human Resources.* 104th Cong., 2nd sess., Mar. 5.

————. 1995. *Child Care and Child Welfare: Joint Hearing before the Subcommittee on Human Resources of the Committee of Ways and Means and Subcommittee on Early Childhood, Youth and Families of the Committee on Economic and Educational Opportunities.* 104th Cong., 1st sess., Feb. 3.

————. 1994. *Welfare Reform Proposals, including H.R. 4605, the Work and Responsibility Act of 1994: Hearings before the Subcommittee on Human Resources.* 103rd Cong., 2nd sess., July 14, 26, 27, 28, 29, and Aug. 9 and 16.

————. 1993. *Historical Trends in Poverty and Family Income: Hearings before the Subcommittee on Human Resources.* 103rd Cong., 1st sess., Oct. 26.

———. 1993. *Children and Families at Risk in Deteriorating Communities: Hearings before the Subcommittee on Human Resources.* 103rd Cong., 1st sess., Dec. 7.

———. 1993. *Trends in Spending and Caseloads for AFDC and Related Programs: Hearings before the Subcommittee on Human Resources.* 103rd Cong., 1st sess., Mar. 11.

———. Select Committee on Intelligence. 1995. *Diversity and Minority Hiring in Intelligence Agencies: Hearing before the Permanent Select Committee on Intelligence.* 104th Cong., 2nd sess., Nov. 29.

———. 1995. *Human Resource and Diversity: Hearing before the Permanent Select Committee on Intelligence.* 104th Cong., 2nd sess., Sept. 20.

Verba, Sidney, and Norman Nie. 1972. *Participation in America: Political Democracy and Social Equality.* New York: Harper & Row.

Verba, Sidney, Kay Lehman Schlozman, and Henry E. Brady. 1995. *Voice and Equality: Civic Voluntarism in American Politics.* Cambridge, MA: Harvard University Press.

Walton, Hanes. 1988. *When the Marching Stopped: The Politics of Civil Rights Regulatory Agencies.* Albany: State University of New York Press.

Weingast, Barry R., and William J. Marshall. 1988. "The Industrial Organization of Congress; or, Why Legislatures, Like Firms, Are Not Organized as Markets." *Journal of Political Economy* 96: 132–63.

Weingast, Barry R., and Mark J. Moran. 1983. "Bureaucratic Discretion or Congressional Control? Regulatory Policymaking by the Federal Trade Commission." *Journal of Political Economy* 91: 756–800.

Welch, Susan, and John R. Hibbing. 1984. "Hispanic Representation in the U.S. Congress." *Social Science Quarterly* 65: 328–35.

Welch, Susan, and Lee Sigelman. 1993. "The Politics of Hispanic Americans: Insights from National Surveys, 1980–1988." *Social Science Quarterly* 74: 76–94.

Whitby, Kenny J. 1997. *The Color of Representation: Congressional Behavior and Black Interests.* Ann Arbor: University of Michigan Press.

Williams, Melissa S. 1998. *Voice, Trust, and Memory: Marginalized Groups and the Failings of Liberal Representation.* Princeton, NJ: Princeton University Press.

Wilson, William Julius. 1978. *The Declining Significance of Race: Blacks and Changing American Institutions.* Chicago: University of Chicago Press.

Woodward, C. Vann. 1955. *The Strange Career of Jim Crow.* New York: Oxford University Press.

Young, Iris Marion. 2000. *Inclusion and Democracy.* New York: Oxford University Press.

Zelizer, Julian. 2004. *On Capitol Hill: The Struggle to Reform Congress and its Consequences, 1948–2000.* Cambridge: Cambridge University Press.

Index

affirmative action, 5, 27, 30, 54, 56–57, 67, 69–73, 76, 82–83, 115, 118–19

African Americans: and AIDS/HIV as issue, 26–27, 122; Congressional Black Caucus (CBC), 1–2, 9, 20–23, 26–27, 28, 30–31, 43–44, 80, 96, 119, 125; Democratic Party affiliation of, 7, 38–39, 55, 62–63, 66–67, 80, 115–16; and federal protections of civil rights, 35–45, 50–53; impacts of segregation on, 21; increased political representation, 64–65; Latino support of Obama, 117; migration to northern urban areas, 40–41; NAACP and issues of, 21–22, 27, 38, 39–40, 43–44, 53, 64, 72, 89, 100; racial group consciousness and, 7, 18–19, 21; racial profiling and, 18–19; stereotypes and public policy, 18–19, 96; strategic group uplift and, 17–23, 122

agenda control, 33, 55, 88, 97, 111

agriculture: agricultural workers and Social Security, 42–43; House Agriculture Committee, 17, 28, 61; minority-interest issues in, 16, 27–28

Agriculture, United State Department of (USDA), 16

Alito, Samuel, 113, 121n

antidiscrimination laws, 40; enforcement of, 11, 54–55, 73, 77, 79, 115. *See also specific*

Baca, Joe, 28, 32, 54–55, 117

Bane, Mary Jo, 104

Becerra, Xavier, 74, 105–6

Bennett, William, 49

bilingual education, 5, 23–24, 46–49, 75–76, 115, 117–19; and voting rights policy, 49–50, 67, 74–76, 83, 117, 122

Bishop, Sanford, 16, 28, 32

Blanco, Kathleen, 1

Brown, Michael, 1

Bruce, Blanche, 37, 52

Bryant, Ed, 110

Bush, George H. W., 54

Bush, George W., 1, 11, 49, 76–80, 106, 110–12

Cameron, Charles, 7

Canon, David T., 6, 9, 57n, 124, 127

Cao, Anh "Joseph," 123

Carter, Jimmy, 30, 47, 54

CBC. *See* Congressional Black Caucus (CBC)

Chavez, Dennis, 45n

CHC. *See* Congressional Hispanic Caucus (CHC)

Chu, Judy, 123

civil rights, 36, 40–42; desegregation, 40; enforcement of legislation regarding, 36, 37, 41–42, 44; historical contexts and federal commitment to, 35–36; legislators as members of civil rights organizations, 21–22; minority legislators and investment in, 5, 15; party politics and, 37–40; roll-call voting as measure of interest in, 7–8, 11; Supreme Court decisions and, 38. *See also specific i.e.* voting rights

Civil Rights Act, 41–42, 49, 56

civil rights movement, 18–20, 36, 41, 43–44, 75

Clark, Joseph, 43

class-based policies, 3, 5, 8–9, 30, 86–87, 89–90, 92, 109, 115–17, 127

Clay, William, Jr., 131

Clay, William, Sr., 70

Clay, William Lacy, 79

Clayton, Eva, 80–82, 102, 117, 118

Clinton, Bill, 30, 49, 54–55, 115; civil rights enforcement and, 63–67, 69–70, 73, 83; welfare reform and, 84–85, 88–98, 102–3, 102–4, 108, 116, 119

Clinton, Hillary, 117

coalition politics, 1n2, 30–31, 38–40, 48, 117

Coburn, Tom, 110

coding protocol, 132–33

Cohen, Cathy, 9, 26–27

Thomas, Clarence, 54, 114
Thompson, Bennie, 2
Thurmond, Strom, 40
time: as measure of legislator interest, 4–5,
    11–12, 15, 19, 32–33, 36, 55–56, 65–71,
    79–80, 82–83, 90–95, 98, 101–3, 106–8,
    111–12, 114–17, 126, 128–30
Tolbert, Caroline J., 8
Towns, Edolphus, 100–101, 109–10
Truman, Harry S, 40
Tubbs Jones, Stephanie, 20

under representation of minorities, 2, 4–6,
    13, 46, 62, 74
unemployment insurance, 3, 42–43, 46,
    48, 50–51, 97
USDA (United State Department of
    Agriculture), 16

Velazquez, Nydia, 3, 11, 24, 46, 62, 71,
    74–75, 83, 117
Voting Rights Act, 41
voting rights policy: bilingual education
    and, 49–50, 67, 74–76, 83, 117, 122;
    citizenship and, 35; legal protections for
    minorities, 35–37, 40–41

Walton, Hanes, Jr., 41, 44, 82
Watts, J. C., 62
Waxman, Henry, 87
Woolsey, Lynn, 92
written interventions, 5, 10, 55–59, 130–31

Yarborough, Ralph, 49
Young, Iris Marion, 114

Zelizer, Julian, 39